D1474121

Other books by

DREW PEARSON

Hail Mary, The Drew Pearson Story (Zone Press)

FRANK LUKSA

Time Enough to Win (with Roger Staubach)
The Rebirth of an NFL Legend (with Thomas Henderson)
Cowboys Essential: Everything You Need to Know to Be a Real Fan!

Remembering

TEXAS STADIUM

*Cowboys Greats Recall the Blood,
Sweat and Pride of Playing in the
NFL's Most Unique Home*

DREW PEARSON
FRANK LUKSA

ZONE PRESS
Denton, Texas

REMEMBERING TEXAS STADIUM

Drew Pearson & Frank Luksa

Published in the United States of America
by Zone Press

www.ZonePress.com

An imprint of
Rogers Publishing and Consulting, Inc.
201 North Austin
Denton, Texas 76201

Graphic images were created by Jim O. Rogers and Randy Cummings and are the property of Rogers Publishing and Consulting, Inc.

Layout/Design: Jim O. Rogers and Randy Cummings
Cover Photograph: James D. Smith

ISBN: 978-0-9796698-9-7

Dedicated To The Memory Of

Tom Landry
Clint Murchison Jr.
Tex Schramm
Bob Hayes
Harvey Martin
Dick Nolan
Ernie Stautner

To all the former and current Dallas Cowboys players who have worn the Silver and Blue and who through their presence have graced the Texas Stadium playing field to create some of the best memories in Cowboys and NFL history. What you left on the field to create those memories will never be forgotten.

A Special Dedication

To my friend Joanie Pieper. Your strength and courage have been a daily inspiration to me. God Bless you. —Drew Pearson

★ CONTENTS ★

PREFACE

After I published *Hail Mary, The Drew Pearson Story* and had some moderate success with it, I got the "writer's bug" and decided I wanted to do another book. My friends at Zone Press, who published my autobiography, were positive about the prospects of another book. However, I couldn't settle on what I wanted to write about.

At the suggestion of my friend and publisher at Zone Press, Jim Rogers, we sought the assistance of longtime Dallas sportswriter Frank Luksa, who was an invaluable editor on our *Hail Mary* project. I came up with the idea of honoring the history of Texas Stadium in its final season as the Dallas Cowboys' home and soon *Remembering Texas Stadium* was born. We decided that the best way to "remember" the team's iconic facility was to compile the memories of some of the legendary players who played there and let those guys—in their own words—tell the story.

Certainly, I'm grateful for enthusiastic support and encouragement shown me by Frank, Jim and Zone Press editor Randy Cummings. I appreciate the help of my new "teammates." We met our deadlines, and I think we've produced a book that will long be cherished by Cowboy fans everywhere!

Foremost, though, Frank and I would like to thank the 20 former Dallas Cowboys players we interviewed for their remarkable cooperation and the gracious sharing of their wonderful memories of playing in the stadium with the hole in the roof:

Lee Roy Jordan—The heart, soul and spirit of our team.

Randy White—There are none who studied harder or played better.

Walt Garrison—A "true" Cowboy; I'm glad we got our one season together.

Thomas Henderson—A character, but one of the best I ever played with.

Larry Cole—The Cowboys' "unsung hero" if there ever was one.

Bob Lilly—A quiet gentleman whose friendship I'll always cherish.

Blaine Nye—He was a professional who always came ready to play.

Jethro Pugh—What a great player and even better person.

Mel Renfro—A blessing as a teammate, someone I've always looked up to.

Calvin Hill—A man I've admired for longer than he knows.

Roger Staubach—We've enjoyed a special bond that continues to this day.

Tony Dorsett—No one has ever run with the same style as Tony.

Billy Joe DuPree—One of my best friends on the team.

Robert Newhouse—Respected for his approach to life and the game.

Ed Jones—A close friend and a tremendous teammate.

Everson Walls—He brought something special to the team.

Preston Pearson—A consumate teammate who revolutionized the game.

Tony Hill—The most effective running mate at receiver that I ever had.

Cliff Harris—Author of the hardest hit I ever took in practice!

Charlie Waters—An amazing player who gave everything he had to play the game.

— Drew Pearson

Remembering

TEXAS STADIUM

DREW PEARSON

(Wide Receiver, 1973-83)

My favorite memory of Texas Stadium surprises most fans. They usually think it is the Washington game on Thanksgiving Day in 1974, when the Redskins knocked Roger Staubach out and Clint Longley came in and brought the Cowboys back with a 50-yard TD pass to me in the final seconds.

Actually, my favorite memory has to be my first playoff game, when we played the Rams at Texas Stadium in 1973.

Can you imagine what it was like for a free agent from the University of Tulsa, who's getting paid just $14,500, who had been "All-Nothing" just one year ago, to be a starting wide receiver for the Dallas Cowboys in a playoff game?

I had a lot of confidence and Coach Tom Landry and Roger had confidence in me. Early in the first quarter Roger called me on a quick sideline route. I lined up in close to give myself some room on the sideline. I gave a little outside release, straightened it up and then drove to the sideline. Charlie Stokes was the cornerback. He was sitting there and by the time I broke it, I had separation. When I looked back, the ball was coming and Roger hit me about two yards into the end zone. I skipped along the end line, made sure I had my feet in bounds, and then did my spike.

I knew there were people watching back home on national TV. They might have missed my other touchdowns because the games were only broadcast regionally back then. But I was sure they'd seen this one. It was probably freaking people out. "Is that Drew Pearson? This can't be Drew Pearson—the skinny legs, the little guy, no muscles. This can't be Drew Pearson."

I caught my first playoff touchdown, and that gave us the lead. We extended the lead to 17-0. It was exciting because of the playoff atmosphere in Texas Stadium. Everyone was buzzing and yelling. But the Rams came back to score a touchdown in the fourth quarter which cut our lead to 17-16. We were concerned. We had lost all of our momentum and the Rams were rolling. Our fans stopped yelling and cheering.

Our next drive started inside our own 20-yard line after the Rams kicked off. We opened with a running play to Calvin Hill up the middle for no gain. Next, we ran a pass play. Roger got the ball, but his pass protection broke down, and Fred Dryer, who played *Hunter* in the TV show—he was the Rams' defensive end and a lot better football player than actor—sacked Roger. It was now third and 18. Coach Landry sent in a conservative play. He wanted to pick and punt. Maybe our "Doomsday" defense could stop these guys; we could get the ball back, extend the lead, and move on to the next round of the playoffs. In those days, all we had to do was win two games to get to the Super Bowl.

That year, my rookie season, the Super Bowl was scheduled to be played in Houston at Rice Stadium. It was a perfect scenario that was starting to unfold if we could just stay on track. It was Drew Pearson's perfect scenario for his rookie year: making the team as a third-string free agent, ending up starting, touchdowns in the final game, and a touchdown in a playoff game. It was third and 18 and Roger called off Coach Landry's play because he wanted to run something else. He said, "It's a two-route play." He told Bob Hayes to line up on the right side and run a post pattern and stretch the defense. He told me to line up on the left side and run a post pattern down the other side of the field. The last thing Roger said when we broke the huddle was, "Drew, I'm coming to you."

I thought, *Oh my God!* You don't think while it is happening, but when I look back, I think, *Man! I'm a rookie, 160 pounds, from Tulsa—first year salary $14,500, and a signing bonus of $150. What am I doing in this*

DALLAS

Drew Pearson

(WR, 1973-1983)

★ Three Super Bowl Appearances
★ Super Bowl Champion (1978)
★ Three-time All-Pro Selection (1974, 1976, 1977)
★ Selected to the Pro Bowl three times
(1974, 1976, 1977)
★ Named to the NFL's 1970 All-Decade Team
★ Named to 11 All-NFL teams
★ Voted All-Conference 12 times
★ 7,822 Career Reception Yards
★ 489 Career Pass Receptions
★ 48 Career TDs
★ Also rushed 21 times (on reverses) for 189 yards
★ Completed 5 of 7 career passes for 3 TDs
★ Was on the receiving end of Roger Staubach's
"Hail Mary" TD pass in a playoff game
against the Vikings in 1975
★ Oklahoma Sports Hall of Fame (2008)
★ Texas Black Sports Hall of Fame

COWBOYS

situation?

I was in this playoff game and the Cowboys were counting on me to make a play. Sixty-five thousand people in the stands, millions watching on national TV, family, friends, everyone was watching. I came out of the huddle and lined up on the left side. Roger barked, "Hut one, hut two." Hayes went flying downfield. When I came off the line of scrimmage, I noticed I was double covered. Eddie McMillan, a cornerback, was on the outside, and Steve Priest, a safety, was on the inside. They were bracketing me.

Usually when a quarterback sees that double coverage, his read is away from you. He's supposed to go to the other side, but since we only had a two-man route, Roger was going to me anyway. I ran between those two guys. Both stepped in front of me and each thought he could make the interception. As they did, the ball zipped past them and they ended up colliding with each other. I caught the ball on the 50-yard line and there was no one there. I turned and ran and it was an 83-yard touchdown pass.

" My favorite memory has to be my first playoff game . . . at Texas Stadium. Can you imagine what it was like for a free agent from the University of Tulsa . . . who had been an 'all nothing' just one year ago, to be starting at wide receiver for the Dallas Cowboys in a playoff game?"

I was so excited running into the end zone that I tried to do this little high-toed kick. It didn't come out too well and I think it looked kind of ugly. But when people like Roger, Randy White, and Hayes are rushing to the end zone to hug you and you realize that you are part of the greatest sports franchise in history, it has to be your favorite Texas Stadium memory.

But to this day, I can't go anywhere without someone bringing up that Thanksgiving Day game in Texas Stadium in '74 against the Redskins.

That game was especially important to me because two weeks earlier in Washington, I had dropped a key pass in a loss to the Redskins in a game that we desperately needed to stay in the hunt for the playoffs. I always felt I let down the team and, particularly, Roger. It was a game we could have won.

So I was really fired up when Washington came to our place two weeks later. That dropped ball had stayed on my mind constantly. I had practiced that same route over and over again in practice to make sure it never happened again.

Of course, the Cowboys and Redskins hated each other in those days. The rivalry was heated and was at its peak. The Redskins were riding high because they were about to win the NFC East and make the playoffs while we had been mathematically eliminated after the game in Washington. To add fuel to the fire, this was the game that Diron Talbert, a defensive tackle for the Redskins, was quoted as saying, "If we knock Staubach out of the game, we'll win the game."

Sure enough, they proceeded to knock Roger out of the game with a concussion in the third quarter. That's when Clint Longley came in off the bench. Washington was ahead, 16-3, but we all rallied around him, saying "you don't have to win it for us, just don't lose it." I'm still surprised at how Clint took charge in the huddle and then took charge of the game. I don't think Clint realized the pressure of the situation he faced. But he played with authority like he was a seasoned veteran.

On his first series, Clint connected with Billy Joe for a touchdown. We later scored again, but so did Washington, which gave the Redskins a 23-17 lead late in the fourth quarter. With less than a minute to go, we got the ball back for one last chance.

In the huddle, I told Clint, "Let's run a turn in and take off on safety Kenny Stone." He liked it and called the play. We got to the line of scrimmage and I saw the perfect defense. I would fake the turn in and Stone probably thought I was going to catch the ball over the middle. He bit on the fake and I could feel it. So I took it deep, looked back and saw this rainbow of a pass coming down in a perfect spiral. Clint had already released it, and I ran past both Stone and their cornerback into the end zone.

You can't imagine what a thrill it was to catch that pass. Now I had my revenge for dropping that earlier pass in Washington. We weren't going to the playoffs, but we still had beaten the Redskins. I remember getting mobbed in the end zone by my teammates. Of course, Clint was the hero. I don't know if he ever understood the magnitude of what he'd done.

Looking back, it turned out to be a disappointing year—the only year in my 11 seasons with the Cowboys that we failed to make the playoffs. But I personally had a great season. I made All-Pro in only my second year and felt pretty confident that I could play this game and have some success.

Remembering

TEXAS STADIUM

HARVEY MARTIN

(Defensive End, 1973-83)

By Drew Pearson

Harvey Martin died on December 24, 2001. He was my best friend. We were roommates for 11 years in training camp and on the road. Harvey was the one friend I confided in and the one I got in trouble with. We played together for 11 years. Neither of us ever missed a game. In the training room and on the field, we were warriors. Coach Landry and our teammates knew they could count on us week in and week out.

Harvey was one great football player. There's no question he is Ring of Honor and Hall of Fame material. Even though he has passed on, hopefully someday in the near future he'll finally get the recognition he deserves. It would be such a tribute for his mother to accept these honors on his behalf.

Even though including a couple of Harvey's favorite moments in *Remembering Texas Stadium* is not entirely consistent with the format of the book, I decided to interview Harvey's mother, Helen Martin, who was kind enough to share her own memories on her son's outstanding career with the Cowboys.

Her proudest moment probably came during the 1977 season when Harvey set a Cowboys record for sacks, even though a sack wasn't an official NFL statistic at that time. He had a great season that year, which was capped

21

off by us going to the Super Bowl and Harvey getting named Co-MVP along with Randy White.

*"I was there when Harvey got his sack record, and he got a standing ovation. He stood out in the middle of Texas Stadium and he bowed to all of the crowd. And everyone stood. It wasn't an arrogant bow. It was appreciation. Tom Landry walked out and gave him the game ball. Harvey looked up, showed me the ball and, of course, I went crazy. But everybody was going crazy because they loved Harvey." — **Helen Martin***

One of the Texas Stadium "moments" that Harvey is remembered for, of course, didn't happen out on the field. It was after a heated game we had against the Redskins in 1979, down in the locker room. Harvey pulled off one of the wildest stunts I've ever witnessed. We captured a shocking 35-34 win behind Roger and one of his legendary fourth-quarter comebacks, and Harvey was really fired up afterward.

During the week somebody claiming to be with the Redskins had sent him a funeral wreath, essentially meaning Washington was going to kill us. Harvey kept the wreath by his locker all week and after the game, well, it was payback time.

*"He was so fired up for that game. That was one of the worst things the Redskins could ever do. He knew what he wanted to do after we beat them. He walked up that tunnel, walked into the locker room, grabbed the wreath and walked right over to the Redskins' locker room. He was going to give it back to them. It turned out that a man, who lived in Dallas, sent it to him to make him mad. If he wanted to make him mad, well, that made him mad. He told Harvey when it was all over that he'd sent it to him. The Redskins didn't send it." — **Helen Martin***

I guess that it's obvious I am very passionate about my relationship with Harvey and emotional about his passing. We were the same age. When Too Tall Jones, Billy Joe DuPree, Robert Newhouse and I are together, and there's no Harvey, it's as though a huge void has been created. But one thing we all learned from Harvey was how to handle something tough. If fatal illness ever happens to us, I think we'll handle it better because of Harvey.

DALLAS

Harvey Martin

(DE, 1973-83)

★ Three Super Bowl Appearances

★ Super Bowl Champion (1978)

★ Selected to the Pro Bowl four times

★ Voted All-Pro (1977)

★ Co-MVP of Super Bowl XII with teammate Randy White

★ NFL AP Defensive Player of the Year (1977)

★ Selected All-NFL eight times

★ Voted All-Conference five times

★ Recorded league-high 20 sacks in 1977, although sacks were not an official NFL statistic until 1982

★ Credited unofficially with 113 career sacks

★ Grew up in Dallas and was a third-round draft pick out of East Texas State (now Texas A&M-Commerce) in 1973

★ The game between TAMC and East Central Oklahoma in the Cotton Bowl on Oct. 18, 2008 was named the Harvey Martin Classic

COWBOYS

Remembering

TEXAS STADIUM

LEE ROY
JORDAN
(Middle Linebacker, 1963-76)

We were excited about going into a new stadium even though we'd had a great relationship with the Cotton Bowl. But the Cotton Bowl by then had quite a bit of age on it. So we were pumped up about going to the big city of Irving with the hole in the roof.

I always thought somebody was being a little tight by leaving a hole in the top and not putting in air conditioning. I don't know if that was the case, but it probably was.

The turf at Texas Stadium was so different from the Cotton Bowl. I loved the field at the Cotton Bowl early in the year. Later in the year it turned dry and brown and kind of like sand. It was painted green to make it look like grass. But it was really green ground and pretty bare by the end of the season.

When we came to Texas Stadium, we noticed the artificial turf immediately. I saw guys tear up their knees because the turf would grab and didn't give like the ground would or like some of the newer turf they have now.

Plus, the turf was extremely hard. Roger (Staubach) and almost every quarterback who played there had some concussions. That got to be a real question mark after we'd played there awhile and saw the results. Roger probably quit a couple of years before he wanted to because of those

27

concussions. It took a toll on guys.

I had a contusion on my hip from hitting the ground. I had to have it drained several weeks in a row. That turf wasn't a favorite surface for anyone. That was one of the drawbacks, but we really didn't think how negative it was until we'd been in there five years or so.

Our team also brought a lot of emotional baggage to Texas Stadium. We were always a bridesmaid but never the bride. What were all those other clever things they said about us? Oh, yeah: We were Next Year's Champions after we lost two to Green Bay, two to Cleveland (1966-70 playoffs) and gave one away (Super Bowl V) to Baltimore. And we were still not there. Those were emotional times.

We sure didn't play as well against Cleveland as we should have and could have. The Super Bowl against Baltimore was a definite giveaway with all our turnovers. I go back and think, my God, we could have finished so good in a couple of those years and it'd been unbelievable history and a dynasty—much more than it was.

Our first game in Texas Stadium was against New England, which had a pretty good team. We didn't play well but won (44-21), and that was all we were thinking about. Later we went to St. Louis and won a close game (16-13) and didn't play well again. After that we began to improve every week.

We had team meetings before we started our run (10-game winning streak and SB VI victory). Some of us laid it on the line about what we needed to do and what we were going to do and what we had to do to win. The thought was, let's not accept the things we'd gone through the last five years and say, okay, we probably won't make it again. We began practicing like we played games—with the intensity of a game. You could see the improvement in the next several weeks.

Of all the games I played in Texas Stadium, two were special from a personal standpoint. One was against Cincinnati (1973) where I intercepted three passes in the first half against Ken Anderson. I was playing a lot of zone and I seemed to get a jump on him when he started to throw. It was just a day where I got the jump on him because he was following his receivers pretty close as soon as they snapped the ball.

On the one I returned (31 yards) for a touchdown, I cut across and took it away from Cliff Harris or Charlie Waters, I can't remember which one. They were always bad-mouthing me about taking away their interceptions.

DALLAS

Lee Roy Jordan

(LB, 1963-76)

★ College Football Hall of Fame, 1983

★ Ring of Honor Inductee (1989)

★ Appeared in three Super Bowls

★ Super Bowl Champion (1972)

★ Selected to the Pro Bowl five times

★ Named All-Pro twice

★ Selected to the Cowboys Silver Season
All-Time Team (1984)

★ Ended his career as the Cowboys record holder
for career tackles (1,236)

★ Ended his career as the Cowboys record holder
for career solo tackles (743)

★ 32 Career Interceptions

+ Also a member of the Alabama Sports Hall of Fame (1980)
and Senior Bowl Hall of Fame (1988)

COWBOYS

> "I believe that Texas Stadium over time developed a mystique. It had a Cowboys air about it. I think that enthusiasm and fan support gave us a definite home field advantage."

(Laughing). That ol' bad-hands guy (Harris) probably would have slapped it down or hit the intended receiver.

Anyway, 31 yards was my max. I sure couldn't go 40. I may have eluded one or two people, and the quarterback was probably one of them.

The other game was a playoff (1971 NFC Championship) against the 49ers and John Brodie, who was really nice to me. He threw a couple that I could intercept. George Andrie also intercepted Brodie and ran it into the end zone. We beat the 49ers (14-3) by those couple of plays.

That was a big deal for me to get those interceptions off of Brodie. He was always good to me. Out in San Francisco he threw me one or two in an NFC Championship game. I was his best target at times.

Author's Note: Jordan made 32 interceptions during his NFL career. According to the Elias Sports Bureau, he is tied for third all-time for career interceptions by a linebacker. The leader is Don Shinnick (Baltimore, 1957-68) with 37, followed by Stan White (Baltimore, 1972-79; Detroit, 1980-82) with 34. Jordan is tied with Nick Buoniconti (Miami, 1969-76) and Jack Ham (Pittsburgh, 1971-82). Jordan still ranks No. 7 on the Cowboys all-time list.—FL.

Why don't linebackers intercept more passes today? I don't know if it's that they can't catch or don't get in position anymore. Maybe it's because the game is so specialized they seem to be in and out every other play. I notice that they're big dudes compared to my time, some as heavy as 265 pounds.

I got up to about 220 pounds and probably weighed 210 at the end of the season. With all the energy drinks and weight programs these guys have now, I'd probably be 245 today.

It was an endurance contest back then. You played every down and played kicking teams most of the time. Now everyone is a specialist. They're in for a couple of plays and then out.

Anyway, I believe that Texas Stadium over time developed a mystique. It had a Cowboys air about it. The fans were so much closer to the field than in the Cotton Bowl. Even the upper deck people were brought in close to the field. I think that enthusiasm and fan support gave us a definite home field advantage.

I hate to see Texas Stadium go. That's why I'm kind of worried about what the new Cowboys stadium in Arlington will bring. It's like the New York Yankees moving from Yankee Stadium to a new baseball park. I just can't see them being the same Yankees because of what they're leaving behind.

There's been so much history and mystique, so many great things accomplished there, so many standout moments in the history of sports, in Yankee Stadium. It's going to be extremely different for all that tradition to follow them somewhere else. Building tradition and mystique usually requires winning championships. That helps more than anything. It builds great memories.

The Cowboys have to finish right this year and next year. They've been on a downward trend at the end for the last two or three years. They have to learn how to finish. They haven't done it yet with this team.

I hope they finish strong and make a deep impression in the playoffs. It would be fitting to bid good-bye to Texas Stadium with a championship.

Remembering

TEXAS STADIUM

RANDY WHITE

(Defensive Tackle, 1975-88)

The honest truth is I wondered if I'd ever *get* to Texas Stadium, much less play there. I had serious doubts because of what happened to me as a rookie during training camp at Thousand Oaks.

I came back from the College All-Star Game and the Cowboys already had started camp, so we came in late. The first thing we had to do, which was intimidating enough, was to run this trail around a mountain, like a little test. To make it more intimidating, Coach Landry was going to run with us.

We started off and about half way up that mountain behind the practice field we're huffing and puffing. Coach Landry is like a train. He just kept going, going, going. You're trying like hell to keep up. You don't want the coach to beat you. It's the first day there, first impressions, and I can't keep up with him. He's running with a limp and beat me by 30 yards!

He was down there finished, looking at us kind of like, hah, hah, hah, as we came across the line. That's when I thought, oh, my, is this the start of it? He beat me in a mile or two miles or however far it was. If the players are as good as the coach, they're going to kill me. If I can't outrun the coach, how am I going to make the team?

When I did get to Texas Stadium for the first time in a preseason game it was so hot I thought I was going to die. I thought, man, I'll never last in this heat. It was the hottest place I'd ever played in my life. I never stopped sweating.

That was my first memory of Texas Stadium—the heat and the excitement of playing in Texas Stadium. You'd seen it on television. Now you're in it and actually playing football there.

I knew what Texas Stadium was. I knew who the players on the Cowboys were … Lee Roy Jordan, Jethro Pugh, Rayfield Wright. Now all of sudden I'm suited up and I'm on the same field and same team with guys like (Roger) Staubach.

You're kind of shaking your head. Am I really here? Is this really happening?

I started out playing middle linebacker, where I never felt comfortable. I knew in my head every responsibility of a middle linebacker. I studied it. I knew what I was supposed to do. But in a conventional 4-3 defense like Dick Butkus and (Ray) Nitschke played, they didn't have all those keys like we did in the flex defense.

Lee Roy Jordan was a genius because he knew the keys. So was Bob Breunig. I wasn't that smart. You had to key three or four different guys. If it was a run you did one thing. If they did one thing you went one way. If they did another thing you went another way. And if it was a pass play you had to look into the backfield to see which back went this way or that way.

I'm used to going straight ahead and just getting the guy with the ball. I'm not used to going through all these other steps. So I was always a half-beat off, a half-beat behind.

A year later they moved me to outside linebacker and put Breunig in the middle. That was Bob's natural position. He stepped in there like he'd been doing it all his life. At strong side linebacker, I could dishrag a tight end that tried to block me almost every time. But on pass coverage there again is where I had problems. You can imagine what kind of disaster it was covering Tony Dorsett one-on-one out of the backfield. I thought again that I just might not make this team.

Coach Landry finally called me in his office and said they were thinking of moving me to the defensive line and what did I think about it. He actually asked me what I thought, which surprised me. I said, coach, I just want to play football and help this team win. You put me wherever you think I can help you.

DALLAS

Randy White

(LB, DL, 1975-1988)

★ Pro Football Hall of Fame, 1994

★ Three Super Bowl Appearances

★ Super Bowl Champion (1978)

★ Super Bowl Co-MVP (1978)

★ Selected to the Pro Bowl nine times

★ Named All-Pro eight times

★ Ring of Honor (1994)

★ NFC Defensive Player of the Year (1978)

★ NFL Defensive Lineman of the Year (1982)

★ 1,104 Career Tackles

★ 111 Career Sacks

★ Played first two seasons at linebacker before being moved to defensive tackle.

★ Played 14 seasons and appeared in 209 of a possible 210 career games

★ College Football Hall of Fame (1994)

★ Texas Sports Hall of Fame

★ Nicknamed "The Manster" for being half-man, half-monster

COWBOYS

Hey, what people don't realize is when I got to defensive tackle they already had Ed (Too Tall Jones) and Harvey (Martin) in the line. This is my last shot. If I don't make it here what am I going to do?

I had an immediate comfort level at tackle. It was like I had been playing with handcuffs on. Somebody took the handcuffs off and said, "Now go do what you can do." Then football was fun again. All the frustration left me.

I knew I could do it in my head. I knew I could hit. I knew I could run. I loved the game. But I was always a half-beat behind. Every once in a while I'd get a good hit and smack somebody when I could just run in there and nail them. But I wasn't a consistently effective player at middle linebacker.

When I got to defensive tackle I felt free. I talked to Bob (Lilly) about this, too. It was like playing the middle linebacker spot and not having pass coverage responsibility. When they passed you could rush the passer. On running plays, if I'm not at the point of attack I can run all over the field and make tackles.

That's what I did. That was my strong point. I could get off a block and run from one sideline to the other to make a play. So I basically played defensive tackle like a middle linebacker if I wasn't at the point of attack and had to play the flex and my position.

You had to play the flex technique because coach Landry made you do it. Once I was confident enough, if I wasn't at the point of attack, I freelanced. I'll always remember coach Landry in those meetings would tell me, "Well, you can do that against this guy but when you get up against a good football player you're not going to be able to do it." After a couple of years, I wanted to say, "Hey, coach, when am I going to run into this good guy?"

During my 14th season I had displaced vertebra in my neck and really couldn't play at the same level as in the past. I couldn't hit with my head the way I did. After that season I thought in the back of my mind: *this may be the end of my career.*

I didn't want to retire. I was kind of like Brett Favre, the difference being that he could still play. I couldn't.

I talked to coach Landry after the season ended. I said, "Coach, I can't play the run the way I used to. I can still rush the passer but you know what I'd really like to do? I'd like to hang around and see if a coaching career would be in my future."

I was sitting there right across from him at his desk. He looked at me and said, "Randy, you have a job here as long as I have a job."

That's exactly what he told me. I'll never forget it. I think he kind of envisioned me still rushing the passer some or sort of a player-coach deal or maybe just going into coaching. About a month later, bam, Coach Landry didn't have a job for himself or me. He was fired.

When he got fired I talked to Jimmy (Johnson). It wasn't a bad conversation. He basically said we really don't need your services. After my conversation with Johnson, I called (defensive coordinator) Ernie Stautner because he had once told me, "Randy, you will reach a point in your career when you still think you're as good as you were but you not going to be. You'll be a beat slow." I'd told him that if I ever got in that position I wanted him to let me know.

> "I don't remember a game. I don't remember a play. I remember coming out on the field . . . walking out of that tunnel . . . every emotion inside of you is alive."

So I called Ernie and said let's go fishing. I was blessed to be coached by a Hall of Fame lineman like Ernie. He'd been there. He'd done it. We became friends over the years and fishing partners during the offseason.

Anyway, we got a case of beer and bottle of some refreshments and went fishing. We're out there and I looked at Ernie and said, "I think I'm going to retire." Ernie looked right back at me and said, "Randy, I think that's what you should do." That made my mind up right there. I was going to retire from football. It's time. If he thought I could still play, he would have said you need to do this or that. But Ernie said he thought that was the right move. And boom, that was the end of it for me.

I've been asked to reflect on my highlight memory of Texas Stadium since this will be the last season the Cowboys will play there. Someone suggested that being inducted into the Ring of Honor in 1994 would rank at the top. Sure, it was a great honor, but you know what my best memory of Texas Stadium was after I left football?

It was coming down that tunnel before a game. That's what I remember. I don't remember a game. I don't remember a play. I remember coming out on the field, that feeling I had before a game. Walking out of that tunnel . . . going on the field . . . the fans . . . the stadium . . . the excitement . . . every emotion inside of you was alive. Being able to go out there and compete. That's my fondest memory of Texas Stadium.

Remembering

TEXAS STADIUM

WALT GARRISON

(Fullback, 1966-74)

One of the first things that always come to mind is that they supposedly left a hole in the Texas Stadium roof so God could see His team play. You know, because of Coach Landry.

The thing I remember most about Texas Stadium was that it was state of the art. The game was supposed to be played in the elements while the crowd was protected from the elements. But when the wind blew the crowd got wet depending on which side you sat and which way the wind was blowing. The only ones who stayed dry were in the worst seats up in the crow's nest because they were protected. The people who paid high dollar down below got drowned.

For some reason I remember the drains on each side of the field. The field was peaked in the middle and water drained off to the side. I have no idea why I remember the drains. I guess I went over there to spit.

Another thing about Texas Stadium ... the field was one of the worst in the league. I don't know what kind of turf it was but if you slid it would cut the hell out of you. There was also very little padding under it. That stuff was harder than Chinese arithmetic. If you landed on it, it would jar you. We had lots of people knocked out falling backward and hitting their heads even with a helmet on.

Yet at the time that was the fanciest stadium going. Now the new

43

one—Jerry's World or whatever they going to call it—is the state of the art stadium in the league. Dallas has probably had two firsts—the two best stadiums at the time they were built.

If Tex (Schramm) and Clint (Murchison) had thought about it, they would have built a bigger stadium and hosted a Super Bowl. There's only about 63-65,000 seats there. You have to have at least 80-85,000 to hold a Super Bowl.

I don't have a lot of game-type memories because I only played about two and a half seasons in Texas Stadium. However, I do recall one of my best games there because I wasn't supposed to play. Or so I thought.

I'd been out, hurt with a knee ligament for three weeks. Duane Thomas was playing fullback and Calvin Hill halfback, and we were playing the 49ers in a playoff. The night before the game I'm thinking, I'm not going to play. Duane and Calvin were the starters, we'd been winning, so why change anything?

Bill Robinson, a buddy of mine, was going to the game the next day. I went over to the Holiday Inn Irving on Saturday night to meet him. He and I sat around and drank two or three … hundred beers until my 11 o'clock curfew.

Bill said, you shouldn't be drinking all that beer. I said, hell, Bill, I ain't gonna play.

Well, Calvin got hurt and they put me in. It was one of the best games I ever played. I don't recall the yardage but I know I made a lot of first downs. The reason I remember that was we won the game (14-3) and since I hadn't played in three weeks, I was sucking air.

There's another game that comes to mind. I was in the huddle when The Mad Bomber (Clint Longley) beat Washington with a last second pass to Drew Pearson (24-23, in 1974). It was basically on the last play of the game and when he called it, we all knew it wouldn't work. So okay, let's get this over with.

Who's going to throw a 50-yard pass for a touchdown to Drew? They'll cover him like a blanket. I thought, he'll wind up throwing a five-yard out to me or Duane and hope we can run for a touchdown. Hell, I haven't run 40 yards in my life. I guess that was the only game Longley had that was worth anything, wasn't it?

I might as well joke about my running style. Everyone else did—

DALLAS

Walt Garrison

(FB, 1966-74)

★ Selected to the Pro Bowl once

★ 3,886 Career Yards Rushing

★ 1,794 Career Yards Receiving

★ 39 Career TDs

★ Led team in receiving in 1971 with 40 catches

★ Rushed for a career-high 818 yards in 1969

★ Returned kickoffs early in his career

★ A "real" cowboy, his signing bonus as a fifth-round pick
in the 1966 draft included a horse trailer.

★ Spent time on the professional rodeo circuit
during the off-season

★ A two-time All Big Eight Conference player
at Oklahoma State

COWBOYS

even my good pal and former teammate Don Meredith. When Meredith was broadcasting on *Monday Night Football* he noticed a player who he said reminded him of me.

"If you need four yards, give the ball to Garrison and he'll get you four yards," Meredith announced. "If you need 10 yards, give the ball to Garrison and he'll get you four yards."

Meredith has remained a good friend even though I only played three seasons with him. For some reason, he liked me, even as a rookie. He picked on me a lot but he wouldn't let anyone else do that. I was his rookie and I appreciated that.

He made me sing at dinner every night for a week. Everyone else had to sing maybe once or twice. He made me sing like six or seven straight nights. Maybe it was because he liked country songs and that was all I knew.

People ask me why Meredith quit the NFL when he was only 31. I think he just got tired of football. I also think it was because he had the opportunity to do *Monday Night Football*. He was like me … why shouldn't I go to work for the tobacco company? I could probably play another year. But I didn't see any reason to hang on to a career that was quickly coming to an end. That's why I retired (at 31).

Meredith wasn't the only one to wisecrack about my running style. Even Coach Landry got into the act, and you remember what I once said about his sense of humor. Someone asked if I ever saw Landry smile and I said, "No, but I only played for him nine years."

Anyway, this happened when veterans reported to training camp. We went through the weight station, ran 200 yards up and back, did another weight station and came to the last thing scheduled—40-yard dashes. Understand that all the rookies at Thousand Oaks were sitting in the stands watching veterans work out.

"Walt," said Landry, "you don't have to run the 40."

"I want to run," I said. "I've been training all year for this. I may have my time down to a 4.7 or 4.8, maybe a 4.9".

"Walt, you don't have to run," Landry said again.

"Why?"

"Because," Landry said, "if those rookies find out how slow you are, and you've been in the league five years, they'll think it's easy to make the team.''

Now that hurt my feelings. It was the funniest thing Coach Landry ever said to me. In fact, it was the *only* funny thing he ever said to me.

I once made the mistake of asking a great coach to analyze my talent. I'd become friends with Darrell Royal, the University of Texas legend, a man I just love. We were at a golf tournament and curiosity got the best of my better judgment. So I asked him:

"The field was one of the worst in the league. I don't know what kind of turf it was, but if you slid on it, it would cut the hell out of you. There was very little padding under it. That stuff was harder than Chinese arithmatic."

"Coach, when I came out of (Lewisville) high school, I wanted to go to a Texas school … Texas, Texas Tech, even Commerce (East Texas State) where Harvey Martin went, a junior college in Texas … anywhere. Didn't you look at my film?''

Royal said, "Since we became friends I went back in the archives and looked at your films. And you know what?''

"Oh, good," I said. "Tell me what you saw?''

"Walt, you weren't worth a s---.''

And you know what? I wasn't. People forget I was a linebacker in high school. I was linebacker as a freshman at Oklahoma State playing under Sammy Baugh. I went to college as a linebacker and might have carried the ball once or twice in high school.

Coach Phil Cutchin came in at OSU, and if you played linebacker on defense you played center or fullback on offense. That's the way it was then. That's why a linebacker like Lee Roy Jordan was also a center at Alabama. Anyway, they moved me to fullback and I hated it.

Well, the fullback got hurt and I started about the last two years there. I still played linebacker on short yardage and goal line on defense. I loved playing linebacker. I just wasn't big enough. And evidently I wasn't worth a s---, either, as Coach Royal said.

I was good enough to be drafted second in the fifth round and got rich overnight by Garrison standards. My dad was making $6,000 a year when the Cowboys gave me a $15,000 signing bonus, $15,000 more on a contract and a new car. They even agreed to fly my parents to watch me play in the East-West Shrine game. I got bold and asked for one last perk: an in-line, two-horse trailer. When the citified Cowboys figured out what that was, and that it cost only about $2,200, they agreed.

So how does all that compare to today's contracts where players get millions for a signing bonus? I'd say like ice cream does to manure.

I ain't braggin' when I say I think I got all there was out of my ability. Of course, being judged as too small and too slow, maybe it wasn't all that hard. But I saw guys who wasted much more talent than I had.

Duane Thomas is high on the list. He was as naturally talented a football player at his best as I ever saw. He was like Gale Sayers. He was so fluid. He didn't do any of that juke stuff like Barry Sanders. He glided through. Duane was smooth and smart.

That first season in Texas Stadium was when he wasn't talking to anyone. We traded him the next summer to San Diego, they traded him somewhere, then a year or so later we got him back. Tom thought he could save him. But Duane didn't have it anymore and he was out of the league in about four years if I remember right.

Duane didn't talk to me off the field, which was all right. We got along as good as you could. We talked on the field, which reminds me of the time he lined up in the wrong position. The play actually was run for me. I whispered, Duane, it's you. He took a pitchout and scored.

Someone asked me after the game if one of us was in the wrong position. I said it was my fault; I'd lined up wrong. I did it because Duane was catching so much flak from everyone.

Anyway, reporters then asked Coach Landry or the offensive coordinator what happened, and they said, no, Duane was wrong. I tried to take the blame and wound up looking like an idiot.

That's the story of my life.

Remembering

TEXAS STADIUM

THOMAS "HOLLYWOOD" HENDERSON

(Linebacker, 1975-79)

You have to put it in perspective that I came out of Langston University. I was basically playing my home games in a cow pasture, and that's where I ran all my 40-yard dashes for NFL scouts.

Walking out into Texas Stadium was like a culture shock. It was like a slave coming out of Africa on a yacht . . . with waiters.

I have to compare everything to Langston because that's all I knew. Our equipment, for instance, dated from the '30s and '40s. The locker room had no shower. We had grass on the field for maybe 20 minutes. To enter a NFL locker room … well, I'd never seen that kind of stuff.

In college I'd wear the same jock all week. Now I got as many socks as I wanted, new shoes and got my ankles taped. During my football career at Langston, leaving the dorm for a home game, I'd go to a friend's room and ask if he had an extra pair of socks because I didn't have any.

Coming to the Cowboys, I could go talk to (equipment manager) Buck Buchanan and pick out No. 50 and try on 15 pair of shoulder pads. At Langston I had one pair of shoulder pads and had to doctor them. My helmet was new but too small. I came from sort of the poverty end of sports.

Guys who came out of Penn State, Notre Dame and other places like that had some sense of crowds and facilities. I had none.

I was just a casual observer of pro football as a kid. We had a TV or

51

somebody gave us one. It didn't work very well. You also have to take into account that when the Cowboys started in 1960 I was seven years old. Up until '69, their first nine years, I never looked at a full football game.

When I was a kid we were outside seven days of the week. Nobody was inside with video games or television. I was just not a fan or an observer.

Did I know who Bob Hayes was? Yeah. Did I know who Don Meredith was? Yeah. When I was a kid I wanted to be Gale Sayers. Jim Brown . . . I knew that name. I didn't have any sort of Texas connection with the Cowboys. I didn't follow them at all.

As a matter of fact, when I came into the NFL I didn't know anybody. I'd never read an article about Tom Landry. When I met Landry for the first time, I think I'd heard his name. But I didn't know *him,* his values, what he stood for or that he'd played in the NFL. I didn't have any NFL history.

Texas Stadium to me was like landing on the moon.

The artificial turf, the speed of it, I had a sense that I could do well on it because I was faster than anyone. But I also had a sort of fear of what I'd considered a parking lot ... this hard surface. It was more like concrete than grass. But I soon learned how to navigate it to my advantage.

So my overall perspective of Texas Stadium was . . . wow!

I have another story about Texas Stadium in a fantasy. After Tom Landry let me go, the following year (1980) I was with the San Francisco 49ers. We were on the Cowboys schedule to come back to Texas Stadium. I made the phone calls and contacts in Palo Alto, California, for sky diving lessons.

In my drug addicted, silly mind I was going to enter Texas Stadium through the roof on a parachute wearing a 49ers uniform. With my luck I'd have made a perfect landing. It was like I wanted to make a grand entrance to Texas Stadium. Someone once asked me exactly when I was hooked on coke during those years. I told them, only when I was awake.

I should mention how the crowds at Texas Stadium differed from Langston. At Langston, we had a couple thousand people for Homecoming. For regular games I think that stadium probably held 500. We never were full. I went from 500 people in the stands to 65,000.

For memorable games, you have to go to 1975 against the Cardinals. That week Mike Ditka (special teams coach) decided I had great speed and

DALLAS

Thomas "Hollywood" Henderson
(LB, 1975-1980)

★ Three Super Bowl Appearances

★ Super Bowl Champion (1978)

★ Selected to the Pro Bowl once

★ Voted NFC All-Conference once

★ 4 Career Interceptions

★ 4 Career Fumble Recoveries

★ Returned a kickoff (on a reverse) 97 yards for a TD (1975)

★ Also played briefly with the Houston Oilers (1980)
and San Francisco 49ers (1980)

★ Texas Black Sports Hall of Fame (2007)

★ Langston University Athletic Hall of Fame (2002)

COWBOYS

no one could imagine giving the ball to a linebacker on a kickoff return, much less on a reverse. A rookie named Rolly Woolsey, one of the (all rookie) Dirty Dozen, sort of caught the ball and fumbled it, which had people concentrating on him. As planned, as we worked on it in practice, I came around on the reverse. Teammates set up a picket fence and I went 97 yards down that turf.

As I got to about the 50-yard line, all I could think about was my homeboys in Austin and my teammates in Langston watching me run. I went 97 yards and for the first time in the history of the NFL I slam dunked the ball over the cross bar. If anybody ever wants to know who did that . . .Thomas Henderson was the first . . . after running 97 yards!

> "I have to compare everything to Langston University because that's all I knew. Guys who came out of Penn State, Notre Dame and other places like that had some sense of crowds and facilities. I had none. So, my overall perspective of Texas Stadium was . . . Wow!"

I think one of the greatest games I played in Texas Stadium is not one that most people remember. That was the week a columnist in Dallas wrote that Russ Francis of New England was the greatest tight end of all time and if you don't think he is watch him drag Hollywood around Texas Stadium. Someone threw that article in my locker.

Well, on the first play of the game I almost knocked him out. I played taking on (John) Hannah and all those great linemen, and they couldn't block me. I was tackling Sam-Bam Cunningham and taking on tackles. It was my finest technical and personally-challenged game ever. That was the post-game review where Landry said it was hard to compliment me, which he did, because it was like pouring gasoline on a fire.

Landry said, "Thomas Henderson is a pro" Looking back at that comment, I started thinking about Ray Nitschke, Bubba Smith, Bart Starr,

Frank Gifford and Dick Butkus. If Landry knew those people I'm sure he could call those same men "a pro." I think it was Landry's greatest compliment.

I will say this. I never heard him even in a team meeting call anyone else "a pro." So I had a game at Texas Stadium where Landry called me "a pro" in front of the whole team.

I think most Dallas fans, particularly the people in Texas Stadium, know of the glory days of Thomas Henderson. They know that for whatever reason, Landry fired me in '79. That I sort of lost control of my life. And then they heard that I started to change my life.

I wrote books, I made films, I did lectures and I built a football stadium and track for my hometown (Austin) kids. I won the lottery, and I still didn't relapse. And I've been sober and helping prisoners, drug addicts and alcoholics.

I think the fans, the Texas Stadium fans, the Cowboy fans, know I had some hard times. They also remember that I was a great player for that team in that stadium. And they remember the nickname.

Most guys were afraid to have a nickname, particularly something like Hollywood. Now if the announcer would have said, "Ladies and gentlemen, Thomas Henderson," the reaction would have been, "Oh, there's ol' Thomas Henderson." But when the announcer said, "Thomas *Hollywood* Henderson," they go, "Oh, yeah! I know him!"

So that's why the reaction I received last year when players from all the Super Bowl teams were introduced at Texas Stadium came close to matching that of Troy Aikman, Emmitt Smith and Michael Irvin. At least that's the way I heard it.

I'd like to think that some of the applause was a gesture of approval for how much difference the last 25 years has made in my one-day-at-a-time life. Yes, it's been that long. On November 8, 2008, I will observe being clean and sober for the last quarter century.

Remembering

TEXAS STADIUM

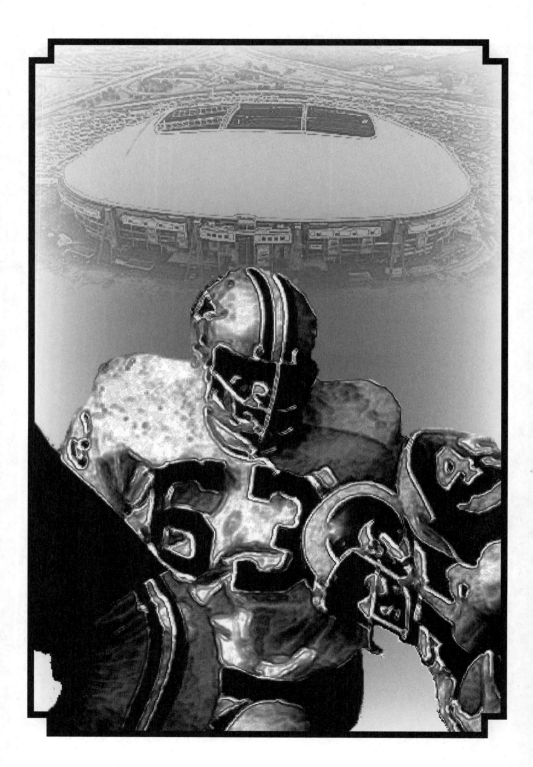

LARRY COLE

(Defensive End, 1968-80)

I remember the first game at Texas Stadium against New England because the field was wet and we were sliding all over the place. We came inside, were told to put on outdoor cleats, and, oh my God, you felt like you were on roller skates trying to play the game.

I would have to say that the old school guys—Lee Roy (Jordan) and guys like that, they hated that stadium. We used to talk about the Christians, lions and gladiators in the context that there were all those fat cats up in the luxury boxes drinking Scotches and we were the peons down there getting paid very little to entertain them. Our concept of football was more like the Cotton Bowl with the crowd sitting outside and involved. You didn't watch a football game with a coat and tie on from a box.

Things have turned around a little bit since then. Now players get paid as well as most people in the box.

We were just the gladiators. We'd run into each other and get hurt. It was kind of like watching hockey. The more fights, the more injuries, the more the perception if you're up in the box of . . . look at those idiots down there running around playing.

That was kind of the initial impression. But as time went on it was like, 'This is a pretty nice place . . . nice locker rooms.' What really was nice was when we started playing games there late in the year. Hey, that cold wind didn't blow in through the hole in the roof. I loved playing there during the playoffs.

Then, of course, as we won championships, there were so many good memories of the games there. Now I'm pretty nostalgic about it and I really, really hate to see the stadium not being used.

I was working as a civil engineer for Southwestern Labs when they put the stadium in and part of the roof didn't have enough support for a retractable roof. It was designed originally for the piers to go straight down but they ended up putting them in at a 45-degree angle because they went against underneath shale and shale isn't very strong.

I understand because of that there was no way you could increase the capacity of the stadium. Being an Arlington guy, I just don't understand why Grapevine didn't take it. That would have been so much better for people in Dallas, Frisco, Allen and that whole area.

I also recall that when they put in the field there was supposed to be another cushion level under it. But it turned out a whole lot harder than was originally planned. The only injuries I got from football were at that stadium and they were sprained ankles three or four times and a hyper extended knee and all because my shoes just stuck in the turf.

> ***Author's note:*** *Defensive lineman Larry Cole enjoyed a surreal career against Washington by scoring four touchdowns—one fumble return and three interceptions against the Redskins. Even more remarkable, he scored touchdowns in his first three NFL games against the Redskins. The first took place in the Cotton Bowl, two occurred at RFK Stadium and the finale, a 43-yard interception runback, happened in Texas Stadium during a 14-10 victory in 1980.—FL*

My first touchdown with an interception covered five yards. On the second, George Andrie knocked the ball loose and I ran in the fumble from 21 yards out. The third was another interception that I ran back 41 yards. The last one was a pretty good play on my part if I do say so myself. It was a screen pass. I recognized it, went out in the flat and intercepted it. That one went 43 yards, and I even outran an offensive lineman.

(Laughing) I think running for a touchdown should be the only memory people should have of me. You could probably do a little take on the

DALLAS

Larry Cole

(DL, 1968-1980)

★ Five Super Bowl Appearances

★ Two-time Super Bowl Champion (1972, 1978)

★ 4 Career Interceptions

★ Returned 3 of his 4 career interceptions for TDs

★ 14 Career Fumble Recoveries

★ Had one fumble recovery for a TD

★ Holds the distinction of being the first player at the University of Hawaii ever drafted by the NFL

★ Nicknamed "Bubba" by his Cowboys teammates

COWBOYS

most vivid visuals that amounted to one moment in time in the stadium.

You think of Drew Pearson spiking the ball and almost throwing out his knee. Harvey Martin, when Mel Gray scored a touchdown, running down there to screw him from his spike. Of course, George Teague chasing Terrell Owens off the midfield star. Then there's Leon Lett's deal in the snow. Some were great plays, some just visuals of eerie things that went on there.

Me running 43 yards for that fourth touchdown qualified as weird. The element of surprise gave me about 10 yards head start. The way it happened, (Joe) Theismann threw a pass, Randy White batted the ball in the air and it hit me in the head. Then it came down right in front of me in my hands. So I started running.

The best part was that Too Tall was going to run down and grab me and give me a big hug after I scored. I thought wait, it's my moment of glory and I can't get away from doing this. I'd scored three touchdowns and didn't spike. This time I had to spike it. I did the spike and even the coaches got a kick out of that when they showed the film the next day.

I also remember an interview after that game in 1980. A reporter asked me how I accounted for the scoring drought between this touchdown and the last one I had in 1969. I told him, "Anybody can have an off decade."

I suppose sometimes the way I played defied description. Coach Landry was quoted as saying I moved in mysterious ways. When I get old and read some of those other things said about me, I know there's one about, 'he has a nose for the ball.' It's funny. I never heard anyone say that about anyone else. But actually it's true. I always had good instincts. My peripheral vision was good. I could see the field and tell what was going on.

I guess the way I look at myself is that I was not an athlete. I was a football player. I had the build for durability. If you could be slow enough your body could hold up. But I had that nose-for-the-ball thing in college.

Bob Lilly taught me a whole lot about reading other people and what they were going to do. I got to where many times when the other team lined up I could feel the play. That play against (John) Riggins, I pretty well knew ... I was studying, too, but I had seen that play earlier in the game and the way they lined up ... so I took a chance since it was third down and the last chance to do it.

Author's note: Cole made the most famous tackle in Texas Stadium history to help beat Washington 35-34 for the NFC East title in 1979. He dropped John Riggins for a 3-yard loss on third down late in the fourth quarter to prevent the Redskins from running out the clock ahead, 34- 27.—FL

The play was a toss sweep and the key to the play was to get the tackle to do just a little bit of hesitation and then the center can block you off. If you know the center is coming after you all you have to do is stick out a hand against him. His strength coming at you is pretty weak because you're farther away. By the time he gets to you he has to go pretty low to cut you.

"As far as the games, I can't think of any heartbreakers (at Texas Stadium). The heartbreakers were in Washington, the first Super Bowl and at other stadiums. But none as far as Texas Stadium, so I guess that's why so many of us have such positive nostalgia about the place."

They ran that play earlier in the game and I didn't get the tackle. They gained about five or six yards. They'd probably run it another time, too. We knew that was a play we had to defend.

But this was the one that by their splits, the way they lined up, you could sense by everyone's stance which way they were going. Being third and two, they probably tensed because they needed that play to put the game away. I got out there and made the play.

If you're Drew Pearson, Tony Hill or (Tony) Dorsett and you make a big important play, you hear the fans cheer. When I made that play it was like everybody in the stadium was tackling with me. It was just an eruption of sound. I wasn't used to being cheered except maybe when I got a trap.

The good part was then to sit on the sideline and watch the offense score.

The next day Coach Landry said if he'd known I was that fast he'd jumped my butt much earlier for dogging it all those years. You know he also once said that I got the most out of my ability, which is kind of insulting.

I can't think of a negative experience except a knee injury from Mike Webster, a center from Pittsburgh. As far as the games, I can't think of any heartbreakers. The heartbreakers were in Washington, the first Super Bowl and other stadiums. But none as far as Texas Stadium, so I guess that's why so many of us have such positive nostalgia about the place.

I did OK for a guy picked in the 16th round of a draft that had 17 rounds. But who's counting? I got a $15,000 contract plus a $2,000 signing bonus. I was in Hawaii and had run up some debt so that took care of the bonus. I used to hate negotiating a contract. I'd finally go in and say, just give me whatever Blaine (Nye) is getting.

Anyway, I hate to see the old place go. If they leave it standing and build a mall inside, that would be the best scenario. Seems to me they could do that. To lose it entirely seems to me kind of sad.

Remembering

TEXAS STADIUM

BOB LILLY

(Defensive Tackle, 1961-74)

The first thing I remember about Texas Stadium was an opening game goal line stand we made against New England. It's an odd memory but the reason it sticks in my mind is that I played most of that series without one shoe.

We held them on first down and my left shoe came off. I'm in the gap, right shoulder to right shoulder with the guard and driving as hard as I can, and to do that you really need two shoes for traction. But I couldn't get that shoe back on because I double tied it with a bow and I couldn't unravel the bow. I knew they were coming up the middle every time and they did. I wound up playing the second, third and fourth downs wearing just socks on my left foot.

I was so relieved when we held them. I thought if we held them and I did pretty well with one shoe I could do pretty well with two. I know that seems like a strange thing to pop up first so I guess it made a big impression on me.

I also remember the locker room before the game. I didn't realize until then how much bigger and nicer it was compared to the Cotton Bowl. We had individual stalls and a big room for trainers and doctors. There was room between our lockers to lie down and stretch. We hadn't been able to do that at the Cotton Bowl.

My third impression was the crowd. We came from the Cotton Bowl where we'd developed a robust, rowdy fan base. We got to Texas Stadium and it never occurred to me that there was a different type fan . . . people who bought bonds.

I thought Texas Stadium would be louder because it was enclosed. When we were on the road in New York, Washington and Philadelphia and our offense was on the field, their fans were so loud our receivers, quarterbacks and running backs had trouble hearing the snap count.

We had the same type fan base at the Cotton Bowl. At Texas Stadium, we didn't have that. It was a big thing. We had it at the Cotton Bowl and at Texas Stadium the next week we didn't. It was pretty obvious. This was a different fan base.

Moving to Texas Stadium in '71 was where we began our run. Even though we were 4-3 we'd played pretty well. We still had a lot of confidence. The defense had worked hard in preseason and during training camp, taken film home to study and was thoroughly prepared.

I think what put us over the hill was when Coach Landry named Roger Staubach the starting quarterback. We had been alternating Craig Morton and Roger and that was not desirable at our level. The team needed a leader on offense. Coach Landry made the right decision to go with Roger. He was the guy we needed at that point.

I know the team captains went to Coach Landry and told him we needed one quarterback. He agreed. Coach Landry said he wasn't sure Roger was ready but he found out he was. We won the next 10 in a row (including Super Bowl VI), which speaks for itself.

I still get questions about players I played against, and whether there was one in particular who gave me trouble. If I had to pick a least-favorite opponent it would be (Minnesota quarterback) Fran Tarkenton when it was hot. He was responsible for the longest play in history back in the Cotton Bowl. He scrambled for one minute, 45 seconds and it was about 90 degrees that day.

We chased him one way and he'd go the other. We chased him that way and he reversed field. We got so tired that we didn't want to be on film. So we just laid there and only got back up when he came back to our side. Coach Landry had to replace all four of us when the play ended.

Sonny Jurgensen was another I hated to play against. He threw so

DALLAS

Bob Lilly

(DL, 1961-1974)

★ Two Super Bowl Appearances
★ Super Bowl Champion (1972)
★ Pro Football Hall of Fame, 1980
★ NFL Rookie of the Year (1961)
★ Selected to the Pro Bowl eleven times
★ Named All-Pro seven times
★ Ring of Honor (1975)
★ Named to the NFL's 75th Anniversary Team
★ Inducted into the National Football Foundation Hall of Fame
★ Anchored Dallas' famed "Doomsday Defense"
★ 94.5 Career Sacks
★ Recorded an NFL-record 29-yard sack of Miami quarterback Bob Griese in the 1972 Super Bowl
★ Holds the distinction of being the franchise's first-ever All-Pro selection, first Pro Bowl pick, first Ring of Honor member and first Hall of Famer.
★ Nicknamed "Mr. Cowboy"
★ College Football Hall of Fame (1981)
★ Texas Sports Hall of Fame

COWBOYS

quick and accurately. It was hard to get a good pass rush on him.

As far as a least favorite lineman it would be Len Hauss, who played center for Washington. I'd get rid of the guard on a pass rush and then Hauss would get about ankle high, cut me and turn me a flip.

We were together at a Pro Bowl once when I told him, "Len, you're going to kill me one of these days doing that."

And he said, "That's what I'm trying to do."

Would my style of play be effective today? I don't know. I'd have to put on a lot of weight. I'd have to weigh 295 to take on zone blocks from guards who go more than 300.

In today's game, as far as quickness and speed, I had plenty of that. As far as natural strength, I had that. As far as growing up with weights, I didn't have that. I lifted hay bales on the farm. You'd really need to grow up in today's world and start lifting weights when you're 12-14 years old.

I don't recommend smoking, although I was photographed puffing away after we beat Miami in the Super Bowl. Here's the story.

I had a friend named Bud Cooper who liked to smoke cigars, and he used to get Cuban cigars from Canada. He gave me one wrapped in a plastic or glass case, I can't remember which. I took it to Miami when we played Baltimore in the Super Bowl (V). I was going to smoke it if we won. Of course, I never got to use it there.

I took it with me the next day when a bunch of us flew from Miami to the Pro Bowl. When I got home I I put it in the freezer. The next year Bud asked if I still had the cigar. I

> "The first thing I remember about Texas Stadium is an opening game goal-line stand we made against New England. We held them on first down and my left shoe came off. I couldn't get the shoe back on because I had double-tied it with a bow and couldn't unravel the bow. I knew they were coming up the middle every time and they did. I wound up playing the second, third and fourth downs wearing just socks on my left foot."

thought he'd probably forgotten about it but he hadn't. So I took it to New Orleans when we played Miami in the next Super Bowl.

After we won the game I fired it up. That cigar was pretty dry and kind of tough after spending all that time in a freezer. I took only a few puffs because I don't smoke cigars. Somebody snapped a picture of me puffing away and it got printed in a lot of papers.

But that thing smelled so bad it was the last one I ever smoked. Of course, we never went back to the Super Bowl, either.

I hurt my neck midway through the '74 season. I thought it was just a crick. But it kept hurting. I got a shot every day before practice, and then my neck would spasm. It got to where I was getting a shot before a game and then at halftime. I couldn't hit with my head. I took aspirin to sleep and that led to an ulcer. By the end of the season my weight got down from 270 to 249.

I went to see Dr. (Marvin) Knight, the team physician, for a physical and X-rays. He told me there were some spurs in there but nothing that said I couldn't play.

I said, "What about the pain?"

"Oh, we can take care of that," he laughed.

I said, "No, I don't think you can fix this one. I wish you could."

I didn't think I'd do the team much good to keep playing. Coach Landry didn't live too far from me and he'd jog by and try to talk me into coming back. I told him I'd be horrible. I didn't think I could play.

Author's note: *"A man like that comes along once in a lifetime. He is something a little bit more than great," Landry said of his first ballot Pro Football Hall of Fame lineman.—FL*

When I walked out of the locker room on Forest Lane for the last time as a player, I took my name tag from over my locker and my uniform. I don't know what happened to the name tag. The uniform is either in the Texas Sports Hall of Fame or in Canton (Pro Football Hall of Fame). Anyway, I only went back to Forest Lane one time five or six years later.

I cried all the way home. It was like losing your family. It was like when we moved from Texas to Pendleton, Oregon, my senior high school year and then I went to TCU and had to leave my father, mother and sister.

I had withdrawals for two or three years. The Cowboys were family.

That's the deep emotion that develops when you've been basically with the same coaching staff and teammates like Chuck Howley, Cornell Green and Mel Renfro for 10-11 years. We had our ups and downs together until we won the big one.

It was wonderful to return to Texas Stadium the next year to be the first inducted into the Ring of Honor. That was a total surprise. I thought it would be just the usual ceremony. Nobody told me it was the Ring of Honor. It was amazing. I got a car, a shot gun and a bird dog that ate up half my house.

Now Texas Stadium is being retired in a way. I hate to see it go, but they'll probably implode it. The locker rooms were so nice. There was carpet on floor. There was enough room to lie down. I remember when I was a senior in college seeing a picture of Mickey Mantle in New York being interviewed in front of a big locker.

I thought that would be what I'd find when I got to the Cowboys. But that wasn't what I was around when we got to that old condemned baseball park (Burnett Field). It didn't even have a door. The rats ate everything you didn't hang up.

Anyway I enjoyed playing at Texas Stadium. I don't like to see it go. I have good memories of the place. Of course, I'll be a memory one of these days myself.

Remembering

TEXAS STADIUM

BLAINE
NYE

(Offensive Lineman, 1968-76)

Surprisingly, there are three things that come to mind about Texas Stadium. The surprise is that only one involved a play or a game.

First was the time I was coming to play and met a Hare Krishna guy out in the parking lot which I seem to remember was empty. He was harping at me to buy a book for $5. I bought the book largely just to get rid of him because I was thinking about something else.

I walked into the entrance and right before I got in the elevator I pushed the button and flipped the book into a trash can right by the elevator. I looked into the trash can and there must have been a stack of 40 books in there! All my buddies had bought them, too.

Another memory is sitting in the stadium before one of my last games there. I don't remember which game it was but it was close to the last season I was going to play. I don't know why, maybe I got there late, but I remember walking in and sitting in an accessible part of the end zone by myself and looking at it empty. I felt like I might not be back because I was planning on retiring.

The point was, I was just looking at it. It was kind of majestic, big and sort of powerful. It was at night ... an empty stadium with just a bunch of blue seats and a few lights on. It was a thoughtful moment.

The third thing was we couldn't get our cleats to stick for about two years. You slipped all over the place when it was wet. They finally got some nylon tipped cleats that worked on that new, improved, extremely racy artificial turf we had bought. I'm sure we thought it was nothing but the best but somehow when it was wet you couldn't stand up on it.

Not many people recall that I tried to retire twice before it became official after the '76 season. Years earlier I got mad about something, said I was quitting, left training camp and went home. When I came back a week later reporters asked me to explain the quick turnaround.

I told them, well, you couldn't take anything I say and chip it in granite.

I was ready to retire again in '75. Burton (Lawless) and Herb (Scott) were (offensive line) rookies that year. I can't remember what my calling was. Tom (Landry) had a little talk with me. He said Burton and Herb were young so give him a year to get them up to speed.

Tom was a helluva an upright guy about it. He wasn't all that bad when you got right down to it. In fact, I guess in retrospect he was a pretty good guy. You kind of miss those things.

Don't get me wrong. He didn't raise my pay. But he said if I'd give him one more year, he'd fly me home after every game, first class, and he'd give me Monday off. That was the deal he offered. I'd have done it anyway since he asked. But I said, OK, I'll give you one more year.

When we opened Texas Stadium in 1971 Craig Morton and Roger Staubach hadn't settled the No. 1 quarterback issue. Or at least Landry hadn't decided it and there were questions about whether the offense was divided over the situation.

Quarterbacks are neat and all that kind of stuff. I don't think the line ever felt there was a controversy. One theory was that we were tired of the flip flops and wanted Tom to name someone and we didn't care who. I don't think even that mattered. To me, it didn't.

I'm not discounting quarterbacks. You have to have one. Quarterback is one position where he hands the ball off and throws the ball. To me the position is not that big a deal. It's just happens to be one that everyone identifies with so it's a big, important position. But as far as that being the leader, not that all weren't leaders, in the pits we didn't look for the quarterback to help us out with our achy jobs and bleeding joints.

For instance, a reporter asked if playing against Mean Joe Greene

DALLAS

Blaine Nye

(OL, 1968-1976)

★ Super Bowl Champion (1972)

★ Two Pro Bowl Appearances

★ Named All-Conference four times

★ Selected All-NFL once

★ Played in 15 playoff games

★ 3 Career Fumble Recoveries

★ Fifth-round draft pick out of Stanford

COWBOYS

was my idea of the essence of the game, the reason I played and a welcome challenge to be measured against the best … and on and on.

I told him, no, I'd rather play against a dog any day.

I've always held a contrarian opinion about quarterback, wide receiver and running back being described as *skill positions*. As if everyone else on the team had a pick and shovel job. I ask you. You think it doesn't take skill to block Mean Joe Greene?

The way I saw it quarterback was somewhere behind us in the line, and that was great. So were other guys and that was great, too. I didn't feel the quarterback was charging the machine gun nest and boy, I needed him up there. Very profound, right? I don't think any line ever looks at the quarterback as some kind of a leader, but maybe they do. I don't think we did, put it that way. It's not that we didn't care or didn't like both of them.

Those were the days when Tom shuttled plays. Ralph (Neely) and I used to do that at guard. Most people thought players hated to shuttle but I was playing so I liked it. It was sort of like getting out there without full responsibility. I was young and getting on the field, so what the hell.

I don't watch many sports but when I see an NFL game I notice how blocking rules in the line have evolved. These guys push and use their hands. We couldn't do that. At least what we could do was an improvement over college where you actually had to grab your jersey.

In the NFL we had to have both fists inside the framework of the torso and we couldn't deliver a blow. You could put them out there like feelers. Your bent arms with fists closed in front of you were kind of like pistons. Or like shock absorbers. You didn't have to give with them. But you couldn't hit with them. You couldn't take a guy and throw him down if he got past you. You had to keep up with him. So it was a lot harder to pass block in those days.

Keeping weight off was also hard for me. On Thursday I used to weigh 268. That usually meant 285 or so by Sunday. We basically ate half the week and dieted half the week. We had to make the weight on Thursday and pretty much went up 10 or 15 pounds afterward. Then you'd take a water pill and get back down. It was like a pre-fight weigh-in. The day after a fighter weighs in he's 10 pounds heavier.

Used to be if a player reported to training camp overweight or somehow gained weight he had to sit at The Fat Man's Table. There's no such thing as a Fat Man's Table anymore unless, of course, they're all eating together.

Oh, there are still some chunks out there. But I think weights have actually come down. You don't see bellies hanging over belt buckles on good teams. I bet New England doesn't have any bellies hanging out.

As far as linemen being bigger now, that's complete horse do-do. You take the linemen we had in those days and they would tower over these lines today without that weigh-in on Thursday. I was the third shortest of 14 offensive and defensive linemen at 6-5.

I remember my son-in-law, who played for UCLA and roomed with Troy (Aikman), came to our 25th reunion. He said he'd never seen bigger people in his life. Only me, (Cornell) Green and (George) Andrie looked like old ball players. Everybody else was in good shape. We all weighed 300-plus pounds.

We used to weigh 300 pounds in the offseason. (John) Fitzgerald weighed 350 pounds in high school, for Pete's sake! Yeah, he weighed 350, ran a 4.7 and played fullback. These clowns who say they were bigger than us … that's all horse do-do. We used to average 320-330 in the offseason before we'd go to those camps. That was only because you couldn't get any further out of shape and get back into shape by July.

Tom laid weight

"I remember walking in and sitting in the end zone by myself and looking at it empty. It was kind of majestic, big and sort of powerful . . . It was a thoughtful moment."

restrictions on us. The fine was $100 per extra pound every week. My rookie year I made $1,400 per game. Figure it out. If you're going to make $1,400 this week and you're 10 pounds over that cost you $1,000. That was serious. One hundred bucks per pound in those days was a lot of money.

When you're a little older you're making more money. But we never made crazy money. Salaries for veterans got up to about $70-$80,000 when

I was playing. That's about $5,000 per game. Knock $1,000 off that for being 10 pounds over from the weigh-in on Thursday, and even back then it was big.

So we weighed what we were supposed to weigh. Besides, if we didn't, Tom would have had a fit. So there was no point in not doing it.

We might have been faster than the guys today. When they decided that players should be bigger there was this whole hog leap. All of sudden you were better if you weighed 320 rather than in the 270s. I think quality went out the window a little bit with that jump to getting big.

Maybe I'm missing this but I think they're playing more and more like we did as mobility comes back. Don't get me wrong. We were still the greatest era ever. You can write that down. Why?

We were big, strong and mobile. We didn't carry a lot of fat. We could move. That didn't mean that fat couldn't have helped. We could have been bigger. I think they're coming down to where we should have been up to back then. But in between they decided you had to weigh 340.

My baby son, Matthew, started two years for Navy. He played at 6-4 and 300-305. He runs a 4.7 or 4.8, left hand down, incredible balance, and I taught him how to pass block without being able to shove. This kid would be a starter if he got into camp somewhere. He's just a superb athlete. All of a sudden they decided you had to be 6-6 to be an offensive lineman. He didn't get a look. It's based on size.

I think for a while they were doing it with a little card. It said 40 times plus height and weight and something about the span between your fingers. The only criterion that's not on that card now is whether or not you can play. You wind up with a whole lot of people who fill out the card but can't play.

When I came to Dallas there were 105 rookies and they all looked like Greek gods. It was incredible. You never saw so many muscle-bound people in your life in this camp. When it was all over five guys made it— me, (Larry) Cole, George Nordgren and the others and we were the funniest looking guys there.

So the old place is going after this season. I don't want to get too worried about it. I said earlier that I took a look when it was brand new and impressive, and I thought about it. It was a thought, a higher level moment.

Remembering

TEXAS STADIUM

JETHRO PUGH

(Defensive Tackle, 1965-78)

The only thing that comes to mind about Texas Stadium is how the move from the Cotton Bowl was so different. The fans as the Cotton Bowl were more enthusiastic. At Texas Stadium you had to buy bonds and you couldn't bring signs in there. It was more or less like a tennis match. I mean, people even wore mink coats there.

At the Cotton Bowl you had the shoeshine guy there. You'd see him on Main Street and then at football games. People like that. When the game was over you'd go across the field to shake hands and because of lack of crowd noise the other team would say, "What is going on here?"

To be honest, it got to the point where we enjoyed going out of town. You go to Washington and all hell breaks loose. Other places were like that, too.

Of course, I never dreamed I would play in the Cotton Bowl, Texas Stadium or anywhere in the NFL. I was only 20 when the Cowboys drafted me (in the 11th round). A judge had to approve the contract I signed because I was underage. Tex Schramm hired a lawyer for me.

Looking back I probably could have asked for a little more money before I signed. I got a $10,000 contract and $1,000 signing bonus. That was pretty good. School teachers at that time were making $3,000 to $3,500 so I was making more than them.

I majored in health and physical education at Elizabeth City State Teachers College. Not so much to be a classroom teacher but because I liked sports. I figured I'd spend time on the football field, the gym, and be a coach or PE teacher. I thought it was easy too, until I got into biology and science and zoology. It went on and on ... anatomy and disecting frogs.

I was aware of being scouted by the NFL. Some scouts came to our games, and I was told that I'd probably be drafted. They didn't say by which team. I actually started getting letters from the Cowboys when I was a sophomore. Matter of fact, I thought they were in the AFL. I ended up throwing the letters in a trash can.

I was 17 then. My coach roomed me with Ike Robinson who was 26 and more mature. He'd played in the Army and tried to give me advice. I didn't want to go to the AFL. If I'm playing I wanted to play against Jim Brown, Lenny Moore, Y. A. Tittle and Johnny Unitas. You just thought the AFL was inferior at the time.

When the letters kept coming, Ike filled out the forms for me. I thought they had me mixed up with someone else.

I played both ways in college but the Cowboys drafted me as an offensive lineman. They asked us if we preferred to play offense or defense. I said defense mainly because I was intimidated by (offensive line coach) Jim Myers. Offense was all that shifting before the ball was snapped. On defense all I have to do is hit somebody. That's plain and simple for me.

I remember people poked fun at my name. There was a newspaper story with a headline that said "Who—Or What—is Jethro Pugh?" I'll tell you what's funnier than that. Everyone thought I was white. When I came to Dallas all the black fans said, "Hey, aren't you supposed to be white?"

I've been asked if I was upset by lack of personal recognition. I never made the Pro Bowl or All-Pro even for the season I led the team with 17 sacks. But it never bothered me until contract talks. Then I'd hear, well, you're not a Pro Bowler and stuff like that. That's the only time it bothered me.

As long as the coaches were satisfied with my play and teammates welcomed me ... guys like Lilly, Lee Roy, Cornell and Mel ... you feel pretty good. I remember when I started I didn't know how I'd be accepted. When I got to the huddle they just tapped me on the shoulder and said, "Let's go get 'em."

DALLAS

Jethro Pugh

(DL, 1965-78)

★ Three Super Bowl Appearances

★ Super Bowl Champion (1972)

★ Shares team record for leading the team in sacks five consecutive seasons (1968-72)

★ 14 Career Fumble Recoveries

★ Twice (1967, 1973) he led team with four fumble recoveries in a season

★ Shares team record for blocked kicks in a season with three

★ Texas Black Sports Hall of Fame

★ A sportswriter once wrote that Pugh was the greatest defensive lineman in history who never was selected to the Pro Bowl

COWBOYS

"The move from the Cotton Bowl was so different. The fans at the Cotton Bowl were more enthusiastic. At Texas Stadium . . . you couldn't bring signs in there. It was more or less like a tennis match. I mean, people even wore mink coats there."

I didn't get upset about being described as overlooked and underappreciated. I finally started telling people, "Look, if I didn't have a name like Jethro Pugh I might really be anonymous."

I did have a flattering article written about me by Jim Murray, a highly-respected columnist from the *Los Angeles Times.* A lot of people sent me copies. Murray wrote that I was, "the best defensive tackle in the history of the NFL who never made it to the Pro Bowl." That made me feel pretty good.

I was playing in a golf tournament in Palm Springs (CA.) with Willie Mays, Joe Namath, Brooks Robinson, all those football and baseball Hall of Fame players, and the thing about it, I was the one Murray wanted to interview. I didn't know how to take it except to think it was a quite a compliment.

Author's note: *"Jethro is one of the best around. He doesn't gripe and complain. He just goes out and does his job. Nothing you can say or do will knock him off his game," said roughhouse St. Louis guard Conrad Dobler.—FL*

Something was missing from my NFL career. I played 14 seasons and never scored a touchdown. That's one thing I really regret. Every other lineman had at least one. I got close once when I returned a fumble 35 yards to the Cincinnati seven. (Laughing) That's where I tripped over the eight-yard chalk line. I think I could have had one but Willie Townes was so greedy he knocked the ball out of my hands.

Some people think I didn't get enough credit because I played left tackle opposite Lilly, who received all the attention. As a rookie in training camp I was standing on the sideline when Bob came up behind me and whispered in my ear, "You're going to make this team." I thought to myself, *it's a trick*, because veterans teased rookies. But I always remembered what Lilly said.

I think about it now when Coach Landry used to come over and say it was up to me to encourage guys like Harvey (Martin), Randy (White) and Ed (Jones). Maybe that's what Lilly was doing. We did the same thing for offensive linemen like Herb Scott. Herb was from a smaller school (Virginia Union) than I was.

No, I enjoyed Lilly. He was wise. He'd been around for awhile. We had lockers side by side the whole time I was there. You get to know a player very well when you talk to him every day. Eventually in the heat of the battle sometimes we could look at each other and read each other's mind.

I retired from the NFL when I was only 34. But I was burned out. I played 14 years and 23 or 24 playoff games, which was like another year and a half. Then the offseason was so short.

Matter of fact, when I went in and told coach Landry that I was going to retire he said, Jethro, no one has played 15 years with the Cowboys before. I said, "Coach, I just can't do it." The thought of going through another offseason program and training camp . . . it was too taxing.

Remembering

TEXAS STADIUM

MEL RENFRO

(Defensive Back, 1964-79)

The first thing that comes to my mind is the contrast between the Cotton Bowl and Texas Stadium, two totally different type structures. I remember the Cotton Bowl and the grass and the openness and the State Fair of Texas atmosphere.

Initially, in Texas Stadium, the crowds were quiet, the stadium wasn't always full and with the artificial turf it seemed like you were playing in someone's living room. It didn't seem natural. Still it was a great, new experience going into a new stadium; particularly that year because we had such a great season.

I came to the Cowboys as a running back (All-America at Oregon) but coach Landry moved me to defense. The Cowboys just drafted Bob Hayes at wide receiver and already had Frank Clarke. So there were a lot of receivers and running backs like Amos Marsh, Jim Stiger and Don Perkins. Coach Landry wasn't going to start a rookie back then, especially on offense.

But he saw that I had a lot of athletic ability. He told me he was going to put me on defense at free safety and see what happens. Of course, immediately, the defense got 100 percent better. We had good cover cornerbacks, not great but good. Cornell Green was an All-Pro.

At free safety I could go sideline to sideline to sideline and fill on

91

the run from anywhere. We had good linebackers with Lee Roy (Jordan), (Dave) Edwards and (Chuck) Howley. We just got really good. I was returning kickoffs and punts, running with the ball 10-15 times a game. That kind of set the stage for me staying on defense until 1966.

That's when Tom called me in and asked if I'd like to move to offense. I said if that's what you want and it will benefit the team, by all means I'll do it. He told me to report to camp the next summer 10-15 pounds heavier. I came in at 205 and off we went. I had a great preseason and averaged six yards per carry.

Our regular season opener was against the Giants in the Cotton Bowl, and I was having a great game. Then early in the game I caught a pass from Dandy Don (Meredith) and ran it down to the New York three-yard line. That's where Henry Carr fell on the back of my ankle, snapped and broke it. They thought it would heal without surgery so they didn't operate.

I was out six weeks until we played Cleveland. I did okay but I wasn't effective as a running back. I couldn't plant my foot or cut like I needed to so the next week they moved me back to free safety. And I still made the Pro Bowl.

It's been so long ago that most Cowboy fans don't remember that I used to return kickoffs and punts. I was gaining more yards than the offensive backs. I heard a rumor that went like this: why doesn't the offense give up the ball so the other team will kick it and Renfro can run it back?

I played free safety my first year. I even played strong safety for Mike Gaechter my second year. The third year was at running back and free safety. My fourth year I started at free safety and played a little of everything. It was about my fifth year that I settled at free safety.

Meantime our right corner kept getting beat to death no matter who it was. They were beaten badly and consistently. Cornell could handle the other side. I practiced at corner all the time so it wasn't a big switch for me to make. It was time to make the right corner position better. So I went over there in '70 and immediately began shutting people down.

But it also meant that the years between 1971-73 at the corner were very, very lean for me personally. I got so little action that they graded me on pursuit. (Laughs) I was grading 100 percent on pursuit. My family would call from Portland, Oregon, and ask, 'Mel, did you play?' Guys on the other side meantime were getting bombarded.

DALLAS

Mel Renfro

(DB, 1964-1977)

★ Pro Football Hall of Fame, 1996

★ Four Super Bowl Appearances

★ Two-time Super Bowl Champion (1972, 1978)

★ Selected to the Pro Bowl ten times

★ MVP of 1970 Pro Bowl

★ Named All-Pro five times

★ Ring of Honor (1981)

★ 52 Career Interceptions are a team record

★ 626 Career Interception Return Yards

★ Holds team record with eight kickoff returns in one game

★ 109 Career Punt Returns for 842 yards

★ 85 Career Kickoff Returns for 2,246 yards

★ 13 Career Fumble Recoveries

★ College Football Hall of Fame (1986)

★ Texas Sports Hall of Fame

★ Texas Black Sports Hall of Fame

COWBOYS

Then in '74, for the first time in 10 years, I didn't go to the Pro Bowl. It wasn't that my play suffered. It was mainly because they didn't see enough of me. There wasn't enough to grade me on.

Free safety to me was a piece of cake. I could have intercepted 10 passes a year from that position. At corner you're dependent on being thrown at. I wasn't getting interceptions there because I didn't get many chances. I'd have intercepted 100 passes during my career if I'd only played free safety.

By my 13th season in '77, my knee was shot. The Cowboys asked me to retire. I said I would but first they had to fix my knee. They said they weren't going to fix it. I knew something was wrong with it even after I'd go see (team physician) Dr. (Marvin) Knight and he'd just tell me I had an old knee.

I went to Los Angeles and had the LA Raiders team doctor do surgery. I was on the operating table when I heard him say, 'Oh boy, it looks like it's snowing in there. This should have been done years ago.' Once the Cowboys found out what I'd done they paid for the operation, got behind me and encouraged me.

I played almost the whole preseason and graded 93 percent, better than any other defensive back. But before the first game of regular season (secondary coach) Gene Stallings said, 'We're not going to start you. We don't think you can hold up. We're going go with the rookie (No. 1 draft choice Aaron Kyle).'

I didn't think that was fair. I said, why not start me and let me play as long as I can. They did put me in the nickel package. I'd come off the bench stiff and with a bad knee. I'd played maybe a half until we went to St. Louis on an extremely cold day. When they lined me up against (receiver) Mel Gray I nodded at Cliff (Harris) as if to say you know what's going to happen. I guess Cliff didn't pay any attention to me.

First, I lined up 15 yards deep and even then I saw their quarterback was already grinning. When the ball was snapped I turned and ran 40 yards downfield. Mel Gray went right past me to catch the pass. I followed him through the end zone, went back to the bench, put on my parka and never played another down until the Super Bowl.

When somebody got hurt in the Super Bowl, they came to me and said, 'Well, 'Fro, can you go?' I hadn't played or practiced for weeks. I got up, went on the field and played three quarters. So I got another year in and got to play in another Super Bowl. It turned out to be a blessing in disguise.

That brings up a question I've often been asked. Which of our first two Super Bowl champions did I think was better?

I like the '71 team. The '77 team was a good, young team that was jelling. But I think those old bucks of '71 were consistently the best.

> "Initially, in Texas Stadium, the crowds were quiet, the stadium wasn't always full, and with the artificial turf it seemed like you were playing in someone's living room. It didn't seem natural. Still, it was great . . . going into a new stadium."

I played with Roger (Staubach) seven or eight years. I played with Lilly for 10-12 years, Lee Roy for about 13, Jethro for 13, Edwards for 11, Rayfield Wright, Howley and Cornell for 10. You got to know them so well as people that it was like a family. Then there was the way coach Landry coached and taught us to be better players and better men off the field. It was a great experience.

I've thought many times what would have happened if I'd stayed on offense. I probably wouldn't be in the Pro Football Hall of Fame. I think with the hitting and punishment I'd have taken at running back I probably would have played three or four more years before I broke something and been out of the league. Moving to defense definitely extended my career.

Remembering

TEXAS STADIUM

CALVIN HILL

(Running Back, 1969-74)

I remember the first time we practiced at Texas Stadium. We went out on the turf and it was pristine. It was like being in a concert hall. Bob Lilly looked around and said, "Can we spit out here?"

Even today, although some of the infrastructure such as bathrooms may be antiquated, Texas Stadium is one of the great venues to watch a football game. Another in my mind was old Franklin Field in Philadelphia. There wasn't a bad seat in the house. Texas Stadium was designed for football. Even in the so-called nose bleed section in most stadiums, it's still a good ticket.

I also remember a practice at Texas Stadium when it started raining. I mean it poured on the field. Tex (Schramm) was watching from the stands, which were dry. Lilly, who was always coming up with something, said, yeah, that's the way it's supposed to be—we're getting wet and the power position are dry.

I also think of how Clint Murchison financed Texas Stadium with boxes and the sale of bonds. He did it in '71 and it wasn't until toward the late 80s that people started looking at bonds, which were now called seat licenses, as a revenue stream. The only other owner who had boxes was Judge (Roy) Hofheinz in Houston. He had two big boxes and he lived in one

99

of them. They weren't necessarily revenue producers.

Anyway, before I came to Dallas, Texas to me was not the south although I realize parts of it are similar to the south. It was more western. I guess my perception was . . . well, I was shocked when I got here because I thought it would look like Abilene. The picture to me was of Abilene and West Texas. The biggest thing I had to get over was Dallas as the place where JFK had been shot. Other than that I didn't know a whole lot other than what I saw of the Cowboys. The only other thing I knew was where the Cowboys played.

So I didn't know what to expect. I was scared to death. I tell Dan Reeves even now that if he hadn't gotten hurt as a running back they'd probably have put me at tight end. It would have been good for me because I would have learned from Pettis (Norman) how to block. Pettis was one of the great blockers. Maybe I could have played longer or not gotten hurt as much.

I'm from Baltimore so obviously I was a big Colts fan. What I remember about the Cowboys is Dandy Don Meredith throwing bombs to Bob Hayes. I remember how Bob was drafted by the Cowboys. I know that on Sundays if we could get a Dallas game we wanted it because we looked forward to the big play.

The Packers were big foes then. They competed against our Colts and it usually came down to them and the Colts, and they beat the Colts in some crucial games. I kind of rooted for this team (Cowboys). They were exciting to watch . . . Dandy Don throwing to Bob Hayes.

The first football game I ever watched on TV was in 1956. My parents took me to my cousin's house for Sunday dinner. Back then, if you were a child, after dinner you were on your own. I was an only child and wound up watching a football game. About the second quarter I had a sense of what was going in terms of the downs. It was when the Giants beat Chicago in the championship game. I remember Tom Landry was a coach of the Giants defense because they mentioned his name on TV.

The biggest thing was when Hayes became a member of the Cowboys. It was exciting that this guy brought the Olympic 100-meter title back to America —almost like The Dream Team in basketball this year. We'd lost it in 1960 with Ray Norton losing to Armin Hary (of Germany). Hayes brought it back and then he was drafted. That was just a big deal

DALLAS

Calvin Hill
(RB, 1969-81)

★ Super Bowl Champion (1972)
★ Two Super Bowl Appearances
★ Played for the Cowboys from 1969-74
★ NFL Offensive Rookie of the Year in 1969
★ Three-time All-Pro Selection (1969, 1973, 1974)
★ Selected to the Pro Bowl four times
(1969, 1972, 1973, 1974)
★ First running back in Cowboys history to rush for more
than 1,000 yards in a season, gaining 1,036 yards in 1972
★ Accomplished the feat again the next season
by gaining 1,142 yards in 1973
★ 6,083 Career Rushing Yards
★ 42 Career Rushing TDs
★ 23 Career Touchdown Catches
★ Career Rushing Average of 4.2 Yards Per Carry
★ Also played for the Washington Redskins (1976-77) and
Cleveland Browns (1978-81)
★ Drafted in the first round in 1969 out of Yale

COWBOYS

because of his speed and the way the Cowboys utilized him. It seemed like he was an instant success.

There was all this great football tradition in Texas with players like Bobby Layne and Yale Lary. Football is important in Texas whether it's high school, college or the pros. You have to cherish that tradition and make sure you're ready to protect it.

> "I remember the first time we practiced at Texas Stadium. We went out on the turf and it was pristine. It was like being in a concert hall. Bob Lilly looked around and said, 'Can we spit out here?' "

There wasn't much NFL tradition when I got here, but enough with players like Don Perkins, Danny Reeves and Hayes. But with the guys now they can look to running backs like Tony (Dorsett) and Emmitt (Smith). At quarterback there's Roger (Staubach), Troy (Aikman) and Dandy Don. And even Danny White, because people forget he went to three straight NFC Championship Games.

There are great receivers in Hayes and Drew (Pearson), Tony Hill and Michael (Irvin). I'd even add Lance Rentzel with them. Look at his stats for four years. He was a great receiver. We only realized later how much that hurt in 1970 when he couldn't play.

Rayfield (Wright) was a great offensive lineman. We also had John Niland, Blaine Nye and Ralph (Neely). I'm so glad that Lee Roy Jordan got to meet Zach Thomas, who's wearing 55 (Jordan's number). The point is there is tradition and tradition and tradition and you just step into it and hope you're big enough to wear it.

It's a tradition of excellence. It's like D. D. Lewis saying that the hole in the Texas Stadium roof was there so God could watch His favorite team. Or like coach Landry saying, you can do that in the NFL but not as a Dallas Cowboy.

I spent my last season with the Cowboys as a lame duck after signing a contract with the World Football League. The Cowboys actually took me to court, saying I wouldn't give them my all. I separated a bone in my foot in the second or third game of that season, took a lot of shots and had my knee drained of fluid to keep playing. I don't think I changed in terms of the reckless way I jumped or whatever it was that I did carrying the ball.

I didn't get any flack from my teammates. Guys judge you based on how they see you practicing. I never shirked practice or tried to get out of it other than the times I was too hurt to practice.

I admit an occasional thought about what might have happened if I'd stayed with the Cowboys. That usually happened when I talk to a former teammate as I did with Duane Thomas at training camp last summer.

We agreed that the things we believed in terms of X's and O's came from the Landry system. I was playing with a bunch of guys who knew how to play . . . Rayfield, Nye . . . Niland . . . I fit in that system. Sometimes I think about what could have been, but I try not to do that too often. It becomes too frustrating.

I don't have major regrets except for getting hurt in the third game after joining the WFL. I was able to meet a lot of good people. I was able to win a Super Bowl, go to the Pro Bowl and make All-Pro. I think about a lot of guys I know who didn't have the opportunities that I did. I feel fortunate that I did.

A bunch of old players were together recently and understand just like some of us hated to go to Texas Stadium and leave all the Cotton Bowl memories . . . the games against Green Bay . . . Now suddenly the same thing is happening to Texas Stadium with the move to a new stadium in Arlington.

Many, many big games have been played at Texas Stadium. Guys who played there played in a place that's a large part of the history of the NFL.

I'm excited this year about closing out Texas Stadium, and I hope we do it the right way. I'm excited about going to the new place. I'm sure some of the guys will walk out on that field for the first time, look around and ask, "Hey, can you spit in this place?"

Remembering

TEXAS STADIUM

ROGER STAUBACH

(Quarterback, 1969-79)

This may not be my most cherished memory of Texas Stadium but it's the one that's gotten the most laughs in retelling. To appreciate the punch line, remember that football was as serious as the Dead Sea Scrolls for Coach Tom Landry.

I always felt there was room for a chuckle in a game at certain times, although I knew he didn't. I learned that lesson early when our No. 1 quarterback, Craig Morton, was hurt and I had to start the 1969 season opener in St. Louis my rookie year.

The night before the game the team met in a hotel, and I noticed Landry sitting alone in a corner with a worried look on his face. I wanted to cheer him so I walked over and said:

"Coach, do you realize that a year ago I was the starting quarterback for the Pensacola Naval Air Station Goshawks? We were playing Middle Tennessee State. And here I am, ready to start against the Cardinals tomorrow."

Landry didn't exactly roll his eyes. He gave me a peculiar look and walked away without saying anything. Incidentally, we won that game (24-3), I threw a touchdown pass (75 yards) to Lance Rentzel and ran for a touchdown.

That was the backdrop of me trying to tease a smile out of him when years later I found myself on the sideline at Texas Stadium during a time out. I was waiting to get the next play from Landry.

Waiting became the issue. Landry stood silently with his arms folded looking at the sky though the roof. On and on we went—me impatient to get the play, he transfixed with the heavens. Landry finally turned to me but before he could say anything I told him:

"I always wondered where you got those plays."

He didn't laugh that time, either.

How I wound up headed to the Cowboys—and stayed—is a story that I frankly stumbled upon. It happened when I discovered that it pays to read the newspaper and keep up to date on current events. That's how I found out in 1964 my long round-about journey toward Texas Stadium had begun.

I was a senior at the Naval Academy when I picked up a copy of the *Washington Post a*nd read a little blurb that said, oh, by the way, Roger Staubach was drafted by the Dallas Cowboys. I hadn't heard anything from the team. I didn't know I was eligible or that I'd be drafted. And I still had four years of military service to do after I graduated.

The NFL no longer allows teams to make future draft choices like the ones the Cowboys used on me (10th round), Bob Hayes (No. 7) and Jerry Rhome (No. 13) that year. Kansas City of the American Football League also drafted me as a future (No. 16) and the owner, Lamar Hunt, came to our home in Annapolis to negotiate a contract.

I chose to sign with the NFL for three reasons. The money was better with Dallas, the Cowboys drafted me higher and at that time the NFL was considered the better brand of football. I received a $10,000 signing bonus and $500 per month while I was on active duty. There were no give-back restrictions if I stayed in the Navy. When and if I reported to the Cowboys they would pay me $25,000 per season on a three-year contract in addition to another signing bonus option: $55-60,000 up front or, what I decided to take, which was $100,000 deferred over a 10-year period.

I gave $2,000 to my wife Marianne's parents, $2,000 to my parents and we kept the remaining $6,000. That was a lot of money back then. I was an ensign making $400 per month.

I never got close to Texas Stadium over the next four years. I spent

DALLAS

Roger Staubach
(QB, 1969-79)

★ Pro Football Hall of Fame (1985)

★ Four Super Bowl Appearances

★ Two-time Super Bowl Champion (1972, 1978)

★ MVP of Super Bowl VI

★ Six Pro Bowl Appearances

★ Named All-NFC five times

★ Ring of Honor Inductee (1983)

★ 22,700 Career Yards Passing

★ 153 Career Passing TDs

★ 2,264 Career Yards Rushing

★ 20 Career Rushing TDs

★ Led NFL with 23 touchdown passes in 1973

★ Heisman Trophy Winner (1963)

★ College Football Hall of Fame (1981)

★ Texas Sports Hall of Fame

★ The Cowboys and Navy have retired his No. 12 jersey

COWBOYS

one year as a supply officer in Vietnam and the next at the Pensacola Naval Air Station where I played one season of service football I told Landry about.

I took leave and went to training camp and had a good camp in '68. I was in shape but I was also fourth on the quarterback depth chart behind Don Meredith, Craig Morton and Rhome. By the time I took more leave for quarterback school, the Cowboys had traded Rhome. When Meredith retired unexpectedly a few weeks later, I had moved from No. 4 to No. 2 without playing a down.

I think if I hadn't gone to training camp then Landry wouldn't have allowed this four-years-away-from-football rookie to be the backup quarterback. But he saw I had potential. If he hadn't seen that he definitely would have gone after a veteran quarterback.

My career crisis with the Cowboys came in '71 when Landry kept starting Morton and me in alternate games. During a meeting before playing in Chicago, Landry announced that we would have two starting quarterbacks and they would alternate plays! Morton and I looked at each other like, what happened to Tom? Did he have a stroke last night?

We made a lot of yards but lost to the Bears (23-19). Landry kept Craig in for the last two minutes of the game. Seeing that I think I'm toast. Landry had to make a decision on one quarterback. It was killing the team to have two. Our record had fallen to 4-3.

The next night, at a charity function, (offensive aide) Ray Renfro whispered that I would be named the starter on Tuesday. Another coach, Jerry Tubbs, told me what happened behind the scenes. Landry had polled his coaching staff.

Jerry said the defensive coaches were favorable toward me. Craig had been hurt the year before. He was healthy now. I think both of us were playing decent football. But the team was divided on who should be the starter. I'm sure it was a close call. To this day I don't know if coach Landry alone made the decision. It could have been that some coaches like a scrambling quarterback. I just know it changed my life.

That was the year we moved from the Cotton Bowl into Texas Stadium. It was a good feeling to be there. The good news from the standpoint of quarterbacks was that the roof deflected all the wind from the field.

Texas Stadium was also a venue Clint Murchison wanted—something different. It was football-only designed. It had fan appeal. They were closer to the field. What I really think is they didn't cover the roof because of the cost of air conditioning.

As far as memorable games, the topper for me was a 35-34 victory over Washington in '79. The Redskins scored the first 17 points. We scored the next 21. Then they went ahead 34-17 before we won it. We

"It was a good feeling (to move into Texas Stadium). The good news from the standpoint of quarterbacks was that the roof deflected all the wind from the field . . . I still have memories of all those games at Texas Stadium. For that matter, I still have memories of games on the road."

had many thrilling games at Texas Stadium but this one had it for all four quarters.

There've also been games at Texas Stadium I'd like to forget. I remember a playoff loss to the Rams where Billy Joe DuPree caught a pass for a first down and got a really horrible spot that ended our potentially game-winning drive.

Then there was losing the NFC Championship Game to Minnesota in '73. I had a couple of passes (actually four) intercepted. But how many times did an interception of mine get run back for a touchdown? I only remember one time in my career. That was Bobby Bryant (63 yards) in this game.

Losing the last game of my career to the Rams (21-19) was another disappointment. Wise guys with dangerous recall still tease me about completing my last pass to guard Herb Scott. (Laughs) Herb was an ineligible receiver so it wasn't a completed pass. Plus, I was trying to throw the ball away and Herb made a great catch.

I've been asked if franchise history will transfer when the Cowboys leave Texas Stadium for their new home in Arlington. I think history will go where the team goes. Memories will continue to move along with the Cowboys.

Memories stay with you. We lived in the same house for 28 years until we built a new one. I don't really miss the old house. The memories are still there. It's just that you're remembering them from a new facility.

After all we're only talking about a place. Fans are used to going to Texas Stadium and I can see how they will miss the routine. But to the players it's just a field. I may miss it to some degree. But there's more excitement involved in going to a new stadium. The positives outweigh the fact that you'll miss an old facility. I still have memories of all those games at Texas Stadium. For that matter I still have memories of games on the road.

I think about how successful the Cowboys have been and that this is the longest playoff dry spell they've ever had—even when they started in the 60s. It's been 1996 since they won a playoff. But I think these guys will do it because this looks like a special team.

Remembering

TEXAS STADIUM

TONY DORSETT

(Running Back, 1977-87)

The first thing that I think about when I think of Texas Stadium is the hole in the roof. Then it's the memory of my longest touchdown run (84 yards) at home against Philadelphia during my rookie season.

We'd gone to a single-back formation. Ours was called Jay Hawk. We practiced this particular play all week and it worked just like we drew it up. Jay Saldi, our tight end, came across like he was going in motion. But right before he crossed the center, the ball was snapped and he trapped the nose tackle.

I jumped off that block and did my thing.

That was a far cry from the way my NFL career began in September before the regular season opener against the New York Giants in Texas Stadium.

There'd been a storm the night before and I overslept. My parents had come down (from Pennsylvania) to watch me play. My parents were my biggest inspiration and motivation as an athlete, and very important to me. I was glad to have them here.

I was up that Saturday morning for practice and by the time my alarm went off and I woke up I was late. My mom kept badgering me . . . you need to call . . . you need to go . . . you need to do this or that. I said,

115

mom, it's OK. Other guys have missed Saturday morning practice. All we do is a walk through and go home. It's no big deal.

I didn't have any phone numbers for the coaches. I guess I could have gone through my playbook and found some. If I leave now, by the time I get there, they'll be gone so ahhh . . . I'm not going to do that. It's going to be OK.

I'll never forget coming to Texas Stadium the next day. There was a note on locker that said, go see Coach Landry. Uh, oh. I walked into the coaches locker room and he asked me, "Where were you?" I said, "Coach, we had a storm and by time my alarm went off and I woke up, by the time I'd gotten to practice everyone would have been gone."

He said, "You're not going to start and you're probably not going to play."

I said, "Coach, I've seen other players miss Saturday morning practice and they've been able to start."

"Those players called and let us know what was going on," Landry replied. "You showed no concern for your teammates or your coaches. You're not going to start and you probably won't play."

I said, 'But coach, I have to play! My parents have come all the way from Pennsylvania. They're my biggest inspiration in my athletic career. I've got to play. They've come a long way."

Landry said, "You're not going to play, OK?" And that pretty much ended the conversation. I ask people, do you remember Latrell Sprewell (NBA player who choked his coach)? Well, it almost happened earlier. I didn't know what to do. I've got to play! My parents are here!

He did play me in the last couple of minutes of the fourth quarter. I almost had the attitude to say, no, I'm not going in. The only reason I went in was my parents were there.

I was on time from then on. He taught me a very valuable lesson.

I didn't start until the 10th game of my rookie season. I was really getting frustrated. I'd come in, make something happen and have a good game, and the next week maybe not be as good. I can't play like that. I have to have a feel for the game.

Coach Landry always had this rule about prima donnas, as he called them. If I hadn't had conversations early on with Harvey Martin, Too Tall Jones and guys like that it would have been tough for me to handle the way

DALLAS

Tony Dorsett

(RB, 1977-88)

★ Pro Football Hall of Fame, 1994

★ Two Super Bowl Appearances

★ Super Bowl Champion (1978)

★ NFL Offensive Rookie of the Year (1977)

★ Selected to the Pro Bowl four times

★ Named All-Pro five times

★ Selected to All-NFC Team three times

★ Ring of Honor (1994)

★ 12,739 Career Rushing Yards

★ 92 Career TDs

★ 4.3-Yard Career Rushing Average

★ Set NFL record with a 99-yard TD run

against Minnesota in 1983

★ Rushed for more than 1,000 yards

in eight of his first nine NFL seasons

★ College Football Hall of Fame (1994)

★ Texas Black Sports Hall of Fame

COWBOYS

he was handling me. No telling what I might have said or done to try to force his hand or get myself out of here.

He called me to his office before we played Pittsburgh and said, "I expected you to be starting my now." I said, "Coach, so was I. I've pretty much written this year off and figured I'll come back to training camp next year blowing and going and win me a starting position."

Landry told me what I needed to do. He said because I wasn't starting I had become pretty much lax, which was not me. Through my Heisman in college I'd run plays all the way to the end zone in practice. But I wasn't playing and I was discouraged. I didn't care. I'd walk back to the huddle.

Landry said, "Show me you care, that you're concerned about things." I'll never forget. I said, "Coach, I wish you'd told me this 10 weeks ago." I started picking it up in practice. Then he decided to start me when we went back to Pittsburgh.

That long run against Philadelphia I mentioned earlier came two weeks later, and I almost got in trouble with coach Landry again before the kickoff.

"Texas Stadium is an NFL landmark . . . that silhouette of Landry walking the sideline . . . the hole in the roof so God could watch His favorite team play . . . lots of wonderful memories of great games won and lost. It will be missed, no doubt about it."

I was late getting to the stadium and still not familiar with the parking. I wound up in Red Parking on the other side of the stadium from our locker room. I ran through the parking lot to the stadium. I ran through the stands where the band used to play at the far end. Guys in the band hollered, "Hey, TD!" I ran through the band and then the full length of the field. The team had already warmed up and had gone back to the locker room.

I was scared to death. I knew I'd get fined. I ran to the training room and got my ankles taped. That was the game where

I had the long run and ran for (club record) 206 yards.

I'll never forget coach Landry the next day. He had this little smirk on his face. First, he said he wasn't going to fine me. Then he said:

"You may need to be late more often."

I still wish Coach Landry would have run me more over the course of my career. I guess it proved from his vantage point that it was the right move. From my perspective I wanted the ball more.

I set the Cowboys career rushing record (12,036 yards) and held it until Emmitt Smith came along. I've been asked if it bothered me when he broke my record. Not at all. When I came to the NFL I thought if I can make it in this business for four or five years I'd be the happiest athlete on earth.

Emmitt obviously weighed more than me. I was only 185 pounds. My deal was always to negotiate, make the tackler miss. His deal was not so much to negotiate but get through those big holes they made for him.

I remember watching Emmitt during his rookie year. I almost jumped through the TV set when I saw this move he made. It reminded me a little bit of me. I was flabbergasted. I thought at that moment this guy will be all right in the league.

Emmitt was a very determined guy. I liked his will. If he was injured he'd play hurt. I did a lot of that, too.

I have mixed emotions about the move to Arlington. Texas Stadium is an NFL landmark . . . that silhouette of Landry walking the sideline . . . the hole in the roof so God could watch His favorite team play. It's also a landmark for the city of Irving . . . lots of wonderful memories of great games won and lost, great rivalries.

It'll be a bittersweet situation to leave Texas Stadium. I hate to see it go, but you understand from the Cowboys standpoint that they're moving to a bigger, better place. But a lot of blood, sweat and tears will be left in that old stadium. It'll be missed, no doubt about it.

Remembering

TEXAS STADIUM

BILLY JOE DUPREE

(Tight End, 1973-83)

I have to be honest about how much I knew of the Cowboys when I was a senior at Michigan State. Is there anything less than not much? To be truthful again, I was a basketball fan.

I came back to my apartment from class one day and my roommate said Gil Brandt from the Cowboys had called for me. He said he'd call back in about 10 minutes. OK, big deal, I thought.

When the phone rang again, I picked it up and said, "This is BJ. Can I help you?"

"Hey, Billy Joe!" Brandt said. "We just drafted you on the first round. Aren't you excited?"

I thought it was a joke. So I said, "Who are you . . . really?"

Brandt confirmed he was legitimate. He wanted me to fly to Dallas and sign a contract. I told him to call my agent. Here's his name and number.

"Isn't there anything you'd like to know about the team?" Gil asked.

You'll never believe what I told him.

"Yeah," I said, "Who's the coach down there?"

I had no idea I'd be drafted. I was looking to go to a construction

123

company and begin an apprenticeship. I watched only a few pro football games at Michigan State. Every once in a while I'd watch games on TV with older guys because they were trying to date my sister. I knew who John Mackey was . . . and John Unitas, Bart Starr, Carroll Dale and Boyd Dowler. I didn't know anything about (Joe) Namath because the network shared only certain teams in a region. Most of those teams were the Colts, Rams, Bears, St. Louis and Green Bay.

Here's how green I was. It took me a whole year to realize we were only one game away from the Super Bowl (after losing the NFL Championship Game to Minnesota, 27-10).

So at the beginning I didn't have much knowledge about what was going on in the NFL. The only thing I knew about Chicago was this guy named Dick Butkus. When we played them I knew at some point I would have to confront him, block him, get out of the way or get knocked out in his presence. My salvation was that for my entire rookie year I didn't have a deep knowledge of all the players in the NFL. If Tom (Landry) said I needed to do it, then that was what I needed to do no matter who was out there.

I knew Butkus had bad knees. I had a crossover block on him and, I don't know what made me do it, I hit him up top. I didn't bounce him or hurt him. He gave me a few choice words anyway.

'You (bleeping) rookie! I'll whip your (bleep). Don't you know who I am?"

"Listen, mister middle linebacker," I told him. "Let me express something to you. I don't give a (bleep). I don't understand and I don't care. If I knew more about it I'd probably be scared out of my pants.

"I know you have bad knees. I could have taken you out at the knees and you'd be sidelined for the rest of the season. You ought to be thankful I hit you up high."

Looking back I see I was young and foolish. But if they had a uniform on and they got in the way of doing my job, that's what I did.

I can't remember being in Texas Stadium until the first game of regular season (1973) as a rookie. I saw it from the standpoint that they have a nice arrangement here. There are nice people in the sky boxes.

My first impression of Texas Stadium was the crowd. I still had a college mentality. I'd played before crowds of 80,000. I thought it would be a wild place, but it wasn't as wild as I imagined. The crowd was more

DALLAS

Billy Joe DuPree

(TE, 1973-83)

★ Three Super Bowl Appearances

★ Super Bowl Champion (1978)

★ Selected to the Pro Bowl three times

★ Voted to seven NFC All-Conference teams

★ 3,565 Career Reception Yards

★ 267 Career Pass Receptions

★ 41 Career TDs

★ Was the leading receiver in Super Bowl XII
with 4 catches for 66 yards

★ Scored one TD in Super Bowl XIII

★ Rushed 26 times in his career for 178 yards

★ Texas Black Sports Hall of Fame

★ First-round draft pick (1973) out of Michigan State

COWBOYS

subdued than college. There were no signs in the stands from fans. It was the difference between watching a tennis match and a college football game.

But I wound up getting into the end zone three times in that game. That was three of five (touchdowns) all year. The rest of the year was blocking for Robert Newhouse, Walt Garrison and Calvin Hill. I understood why the Cowboys drafted me. I could block and they were run-oriented. What they didn't know was that I could catch the football.

The stadium itself began to have an atmosphere that motivated you. I think it was a year or so later that they decided to let fans bring in their signs. That's when fans started to get rowdy. They began clapping, cheering and throwing things around.

Spartan Stadium had a field built like Texas Stadium with a high crown. The turf was actually about the same. So I was comfortable from that standpoint.

Texas Stadium at that time was one of the premier facilities in the NFL. It had more character than most stadiums and its own distinct identity. There wasn't another stadium in the league that had a hole in the roof. That hole in the roof was a great advantage for the home team and a great disadvantage for the visiting team if they played a 12 or 3 o'clock game because the sun would sit on their bench and fry 'em. By the time they got to the fourth quarter they were drained from just sitting on the sidelines.

I loved playing in that stadium because of the fans. Over the years we became America's Team and then God's team because He could watch His favorite team play through that hole in the roof. The stadium had lots of character and brought another dimension to the aura the Cowboys seemed to possess anyway. The players played well. The stadium served them well. The tunnel leading to the field at Texas Stadium had more impact and influence than any stadium I played in. You felt the momentum and adrenalin coming at you with each step.

I'm sure all the fans will miss the stadium as much as the players who played there. They were die-hard fans. I think they'll be a little sad because it's my understanding that they're going to implode the facility. There'll probably be a congregation standing on the other side of Highway 114 when it happens, watching the proceedings, taking pictures and crying at the same time.

I also think of people who fly to Dallas from other parts of the country. I've been on lots of flights and the first thing I hear them say when we're coming in is, "Hey, is that Texas Stadium down there?"

Texas Stadium was a great venue. It became more of a landmark up close than far away. I'm going to miss it not being there. There wasn't a lot going on in the city when it was built. The stadium held the city together quite a bit because it was a gathering place for people in the Metroplex.

I think Jerry Jones realizes that he doesn't own the Cowboys. He just bought them. The city of Irving never owned Texas Stadium. Irving just happened to have the land to put it on. That stadium belongs to the fans.

> "The stadium had lots of character and brought another dimension to the aura the Cowboys seemed to possess . . . The tunnel leading to the field at Texas Stadium had more impact and influence than any other stadium I played in. You felt the momentum and adrenalin coming at you with each step."

Remembering

TEXAS STADIUM

ROBERT NEWHOUSE

(Fullback, 1972-83)

Like any young kid from the country I had the usual dreams of playing football in high school, maybe someday in college and maybe even someday in the NFL. But my dream was sort of reversed toward playing for the Cowboys.

Growing up in Hallsville, 135 miles east of Dallas, you turned on the black and white television and all you saw was the Cowboys team, the players, the whole era. My dream turned a little negative toward the Cowboys because everything you saw was Cowboys, including the star.

I wanted to be a little Kansas City Chief because of the mini-backs like (5-9,200) Mike Garrett and (5-10, 182) Warren McVea they had then. I was always teased about my size (listed at 5-10, 210). So I wanted to go somewhere where I fit and hopefully I could make it there. Maybe I fit better in that kind of platoon.

As life would have it, it wasn't to be. I had a decent career at the University of Houston (2,961 yards, 6.4 per carry average, 19 touchdowns) toward the end of my years there. My beginning wasn't that good. I wasn't allowed to play for a lot of different reasons.

I remember the day I was drafted by the Cowboys in the second round. I was riding around with one of my former teammates when they made the announcement. I felt a little disappointed because I wanted to go

131

far away from home. Playing at Houston and being in Texas all my life I wanted to play for Kansas City. I thought, here I go again. I'm stuck in Dallas which is only 135 miles from my home town. I should have felt a lot of excitement because I just wanted to play at the NFL level and prove to people that I could do it.

A reporter from Dallas asked me if I felt my lack of height was a handicap. Here's what I told him:

"I'm not going to grow an inch, but maybe I can play a little bigger than I am."

I had the luxury of beginning my NFL tour at Texas Stadium. In college at the University of Houston, I played in the Astrodome, the Eighth Wonder of the World. I came to Dallas as a pro football player and here's Texas Stadium, the hole in the roof, the whole nine yards, lots of publicity about it. It's a new beginning, a new era. The Cowboys had just won the Super Bowl.

I used to go to that stadium before I made the team and think about playing there. It was one of those spectacles, like a dream come true. Playing in Texas Stadium, practicing in Texas Stadium on rainy days, meeting all the players I played with—was another dream come true. I was in awe from that day on.

But to cap if off, that facility was like you go in and have your own home. I felt comfortable there. I felt as though I played 12 years in the NFL in my house.

I remember clear as day the first time I went down the tunnel leading to the field. The slope of the tunnel throws you forward as you walk. The anticipation of going out there produces a feeling of awe. The first day I walked out there and looked up I thought I'd died and gone to heaven. To walk out to a full stadium, the crowd roaring was a great feeling. It gave me a feeling of success and emotion to come down the roller coaster on that slope, walk into those wide open spaces and into a roaring crowd.

My pre-game ritual was in believing, for whatever it was worth, that we would never lose a game at home. I don't know what our winning percentage at home was but because of that stadium there was a comfort zone. The crowd was behind you, you'd hear your name called . . . it was all good. Playing in that stadium was a unique experience for me.

Before each and every game I rehearsed my job. People said when

DALLAS

Robert Newhouse

(RB, 1972-1983)

★ Four Super Bowl Appearances

★ Two-time Super Bowl Champion (1972, 1978)

★ 4,784 Career Yards Rushing

★ Led the team in rushing in 1975 with 930 yards

★ 31 Career Rushing TDs

★ 956 Career Yards Receiving

★ 120 Career Receptions

★ 5 Career Receiving TDs

★ Threw a 29-yard TD pass to Golden Richards against Denver
in Super Bowl XII

★ Texas Black Sports Hall of Fame

★ In 1972 when the College All-Stars played the previous year's
Super Bowl champion, Newhouse scored a TD
against the Cowboys

★ Continues to work for the Cowboys in Alumni Affairs

COWBOYS

you went on the field you needed to concentrate. I did all that during the week in practice. I made a concentrated effort to know my assignments. So when the game started I reacted. Hopefully I went the right way and did the right thing. Of course, I had three years to sit on the bench and figure that out.

"I remember clear as day the first time I went down the tunnel leading to the field. The anticipation of going out there produces a feeling of awe. The first day I walked out there and looked up, I thought I had died and gone to heaven. To walk out to a full stadium, the crowd roaring, was a great feeling."

One memory that stands out isn't from one of my best games. It was the time I broke a run for 54 yards. I still remember to this day that I ran 54 yards, the longest of my career, in that stadium. No, it wasn't a touchdown. Another thing I realized and accepted after running 54 yards. I wasn't a long distance runner.

I had a quick burst. When I broke out I just knew I was going to score but about four or five guys caught me. Three of them were linemen.

There's another odd highlight from a game against Washington. It was a third down play, and I was just trying to get a first down. I scored on this one although someone hit me before I crossed the goal line and my helmet flew off. I'm in for the score when the officials say to bring the ball back and spot it where I lost my helmet because it was an unsafe play. Back in that day the play ended where equipment came off. That's not the case now.

I also think about a game against San Francisco late in my career. I was promoted or demoted—whatever it was I was still on the team—to a kickoff coverage guy. When a coach told me to run down on a kickoff I thought he was talking to someone else. I went down, made the tackle and the guy fumbled the ball to us. I have my private days when I go down memory lane.

One last thing I remember was the shadow and shade at Texas Stadium when we played the New York Giants. The sun would shine on the visitor's side. Our side always caught a little bit of shade. I knew a couple of guys on the Giants and could see they were dying. As the game went on I always checked to see how the sun had heated up the other side. The shadow on the stadium was like the closing of a sunset.

Early on, Texas Stadium was kind of a formal setting as far as the way the fans dressed. Now it's come as you go. Games at Texas Stadium back then were a day to be reckoned with because the city thrived on winning and losing with the Cowboys. You won a game and you could go anywhere and do anything in the city and everyone knew who you were. It was the Grand 'Ole Opry days.

I was an admirer and in awe of the players I played with. My biggest win at Texas Stadium was the first one. There were lots of games we won to go on into championships but to me personally my greatest win was the first. I don't think I even played in the game. I may have gotten in a few plays.

But it started a desire within me to be part of a team that won. I was fortunate to stay with the organization, the Dallas Cowboys, Texas Stadium and my home field for 12 successful years.

It's all a big blur now. Soon everything will be overtaken by the past because the whole facility will be blown up. But that's part of life. Texas Stadium was where I began and where I ended my playing days. It was a part of me. A lot of my teammates helped build that place. Facilities come and go. So do statues. But the memories will always be there.

Everything good must come to an end. The closing of Texas Stadium will definitely cast a shadow.

Remembering

TEXAS STADIUM

ED "TOO TALL" JONES

(Defensive End, 1974-78, 1980-89)

In Tennessee we got to see TV games of the Cowboys and St. Louis Cardinals, which are the Arizona Cardinals now. We saw more of the Cowboys because they were winning. So I grew up as a Cowboy fan.

My senior year at Tennessee State I was blessed enough to be invited to play in the East-West Shrine game in San Francisco. Cornell Green was scouting for the Cowboys in the offseason and he'd been to our campus numerous times. The Cowboys were looking at me and my teammate, Waymond Bryant, a linebacker who later played for the Chicago Bears.

After the game, Red Hickey, another Dallas scout, invited us to the NFC Championship Game in Texas Stadium between the Cowboys and Minnesota Vikings. First of all, it was the nicest facility I ever set foot in. I was honored to be there.

Abner Haynes was our host. We had the opportunity the night before the game to meet Rodrigo Barnes and Harvey Martin. I knew about both of them. I was honored to be introduced. Unfortunately, Dallas didn't win that game.

They were taking us back to the hotel on the players' bus after the game, and I was one of the first to board. Tom and Alicia (Landry) were already sitting there. I remember Tom Landry asking me questions about the East-West game. I couldn't believe it. Here's a man who just coached a Championship game and he'd watched me play in the East-West. I was very impressed with my first experience at Texas Stadium.

I didn't start as rookie. Pat Toomay started. I only played passing downs. Harvey and I were called Thunder and Lightning. I would come in for Toomay and Harvey would replace Larry Cole. I don't know if I was more excited about playing for the Cowboys in my first game or playing with teammates that I had watched growing up as a kid. I was probably more in awe of them than the uniform or playing before all the wonderful fans we had.

There was a lot of pressure on me as a No. 1 pick. Bob Lilly and Jethro Pugh sat me down and said (defensive coach) Ernie Stautner has gone over a lot of things with you. We got your back. So just get after the football. I remind them every time I see them that they got an elephant off my back.

I was a typical rookie feeling a lot of pressure trying to learn a new system. I'd never played before a crowd like that. The Cowboys had training camp practices at Thousand Oaks where there were more people in the stands than at Tennessee State games. I was in awe with that. I wanted to do extremely well. I didn't want to disappoint myself, family, friends, Tennessee State, and most of all, my teammates and Tom Landry.

I remember a game where we beat Chicago 10-9 (in 1981) where I blocked their extra point, which was the difference in the game. But if I had to pick one memorable game it would be the 1977 divisional playoff against the Bears. Walter Payton was in his heyday. I knew Payton. We'd made an All-America team together. Payton was by far the best running back in the league at that time. We knew we had to stop him to beat them.

I had a good game, particularly against the run (five unassisted tackles). We shut down Payton (60 yards rushing), won the game (37-7) and were on our way to winning the Super Bowl.

Having played 15 years, I have so many fond memories. That one ranked with the best along with the year (1985) we beat the New York Giants (28-21). I tipped two Phil Simms passes and Jim Jeffcoat ran one back (65 yards) for a touchdown to clinch the division title. I've never seen players so excited for that game, and I don't know why. It seemed like the excitement was far beyond anything I'd ever experienced.

DALLAS

Ed "Too Tall" Jones

(DL, 1974-78, 1980-89)

★ Three Super Bowl Appearances

★ Super Bowl Champion (1978)

★ Selected to the Pro Bowl three times

★ Named All-Pro twice

★ Unofficial sack total of 106 for 15 years

★ After sacks became an official NFL statistic in 1982, he was credited with 57 "official" career sacks

★ 3 Career Interceptions

★ Shares team record for blocks in a season with three

★ 7 Career Blocked Field Goals

★ Missed the 1979 season after retiring to pursue a boxing career

★ Texas Black Sports Hall of Fame

★ One of just three players to log 15 seasons with the Cowboys

★ Nicknamed "Too Tall" because of his 6'9" height

COWBOYS

During all those years, I always felt we were the best conditioned team. Why? We trained in Thousand Oaks, California, where we could actually work out. We weren't just trying to survive the heat like a lot of teams that trained in places that were extremely hot. We had our legs. We were in great shape. We knew that going into those games. So we knew we had an advantage there over our opponents. As for me personally, I loved playing on that turf compared to other stadiums.

> "After the East-West Shrine Game, (the Cowboys) invited us to the NFC Championship game in Texas Stadium between the Cowboys and Minnesota Vikings. It was the nicest facility I'd ever set foot in. I was honored to be there."

Another advantage about playing at home was the 12th man in the stands. I always felt our fans were good to us. Even though I was never one to look in the stands I knew my friends and family were there to watch me. That was the biggest advantage we had. Fans were right on top of things. Trust me, from talking to players around the league, they felt that.

I also remember those three o'clock kickoffs where the sun settled on the other team's bench. One of the funniest things I ever saw was a year we were playing the Giants and they were being roasted by the sun. I saw John Mendenhall and Harry Carson telling their players to come on to the other side of the field. They all took their helmets off and dropped to a knee in the shade.

Along with the good comes the bad. The most depressed I've ever been in my life was when we played the Bears in 1985. The whipping (44-0) we took . . . it was like we were helpless and there was nothing we could do. After the game, talking to my teammates, I said, guys we don't ever want to experience anything like that ever again.

I've never talked much about why I retired from the Cowboys in 1979 to become a professional boxer. I had a 6-0 record when I decided to return to the NFL after an absence of one year. When Harvey Martin was writing his book, *Texas Thunder*, he asked me to describe the fight game.

"Tougher than football," I told him. "You have no pads in the ring."

Harvey wanted to know why I quit if I was unbeaten. I said it was because of a shoulder injury I suffered at Tennessee State.

"I can't throw an overhead right," I said. "(Larry) Holmes and (Gerry) Cooney would kill me because of that."

I want to share a final memory about an opponent rather than Texas Stadium. I'm reminded of Hall of Fame offensive tackle Dan Dierdorf of the St. Louis Cardinals every time I see players jabbering at each other. I went head-up against Dierdorf for eight seasons and it wasn't until the last year that we ever exchanged a word. Both of us held to a higher code of professional conduct.

There came a game day in St. Louis where Dierdorf took his stance in front of me for the first play of the game. Before the ball was snapped, he spoke. I answered and this was the extent of our conversation over a period of eight years.

"I'm retiring," he said.

"I know. I'm glad," I said.

Remembering

TEXAS STADIUM

EVERSON WALLS

(Cornerback, 1981-89)

My first fantasy about playing in Texas Stadium took place in 1972 when I was 12 years old and my uncle took me to a playoff game there. We didn't have a lot of money so our tickets were almost at the top of the stadium. I remember birds and pigeons up on the roof. We were practically in a pigeon coop. That's how high we were.

I'd been to the Astrodome in Houston with my grandparents and I remembered all of the different colored seats there. I thought Texas Stadium was unusual in comparison because there was a big hole in the roof. I didn't understand why. I thought they'd close it.

I didn't have a chance to get any autographs after the game but just going to the game made me think of being a professional player. At the time I was a little hotshot football player. I was the best running back on my sixth grade team. I had no dreams of being a defensive back. All my dreams were about scoring touchdowns as a running back in the NFL.

Calvin Hill was a player I looked up to because of the way he jumped over tacklers. He was one of the bigger running backs I'd seen. I was also one of the bigger players for my age. I considered myself the Calvin Hill of my Razorbacks little league team.

It was a given that I fantasized about playing for the Cowboys. I went to high school at Richardson Berkner and lived only two miles from the Cowboys old practice field on Forest Lane.

I used to ride my bike to watch them practice. It was no big deal to pedal a couple of miles to see the players work out. We used to go up there all the time and hang over the tin fence. I remember (receiver) Otto Stowe because he was one of the stars. His Afro was almost as big as Drew Pearson's.

I had three choices as a free agent after the draft. I had offers from the Cowboys, Buffalo and New Orleans. The Saints were the Aint's at that time, losing so much that their fans were wearing bags over their heads. Obviously, I didn't want to go there. I was used to winning at Grambling. Everywhere we went we were considered the toast of the town. We played in big arenas. Being a Texas boy, there was no way I was going up there and play in cold Buffalo.

So it was a no-brainer for me. My senior year at Grambling I'd seen a Cowboys playoff game against Atlanta (Dallas won, 30-28). But (receivers) Alfred Jenkins and Walter Francis, and tight end Jim Mitchell and (quarterback) Steve Bartkowski were killing the Cowboys. I remember hearing on TV that the Cowboys were weak at the defensive back position. So I thought, "Hmmm, these guys need some help at DB."

So that was it. I'd go to my hometown team that needed a position I could play well. Yet I was still mad over the fact they didn't think I was good enough to draft. Not only was I a Black College All-America. I was a Division I-AA All-America, which was chosen for all small colleges. That was a disappointment and I used it for motivation. The way I heard it later I was supposedly too slow to play in an NFL secondary.

I can still recall the first time I played at Texas Stadium in a preseason game. You know, when you are watching NFL Films and they use a camera with a wide aperture and everything looks that much wider . . . that's what it was like. You come down that tunnel and everything just opens up. There weren't that many people in the stands for pre-game warm-up so the first thing I did was walk beneath that hole in the roof, look up and focused on the void. I was nervous, very nervous.

I was nervous just being on the bus going to the stadium. I tried to focus on what I had to do. It's the way I played my whole career. You had to think so much in the Cowboys system that you couldn't get caught up talking trash and all that peripheral stuff. Gene Stallings (defensive backs coach) ruled with an iron hand and made sure you knew all your assignments.

DALLAS

Everson Walls

(DB, 1981-1993)

★ Two Super Bowl Appearances

★ Super Bowl Champion (1991)

★ Selected to the Pro Bowl four times

★ Named All-Pro four times

★ NFL Defensive Back of the Year (1982)

★ Led the NFL in interceptions in 1981 (11), 1982 (7) and 1985 (9)

★ 57 Career Interceptions

★ Led the Cowboys in interceptions a team-record five times

★ Only player to lead the NFL in interceptions three times

★ Also played for the New York Giants (1990-92) and Cleveland Browns (1992-93)

★ Shares the Pro Bowl record of four interceptions

★ Southwestern Athletic Conference Hall of Fame (2006)

★ Louisiana Sports Hall of Fame (1998)

★ Texas Black Sports Hall of Fame (2003)

COWBOYS

My main thought was how to play my assignments, if I even got into the game. I'd seen preseason games before where sometimes guys don't even get a chance to play. I just wanted a chance to get into the game. I got in and made a play. But it wasn't an interception like you might think.

By now I knew that (defensive coaches) Ernie Stautner, Jerry Tubbs and Stallings had fallen in love with Michael Downs, a free agent safety from Rice. Mike was like Spiderman or Plastic Man with long arms and legs. He was quiet, focused and smart. You could tell the coaches had plans for this guy.

I was always opportunistic. So I got on the punt block team with Mike. He broke through and blocked a punt. I was right there. The ball didn't take any funny bounces. It hit flat on the ground, bounced into the air just like it levitated. I picked up that joker and scored.

That was kind of a foretelling of how it went with us in later years. Mike did all the hard work and I got the glory. Mike would call the defense and make 10-12 hard tackles that nobody really appreciated. Then I'd come up with a couple of interceptions which was more glamorous.

> "I never had any problems with the sun or the high crown on the Texas Stadium field. I always loved playing on artificial turf because it made me feel fast. It was like when you were a kid and you put on those Pro Keds and all of a sudden they made you feel faster. That's what it was like at Texas Stadium."

I never had any problems with the sun or the high crown on the Texas Stadium field. I knew where the traps were because I'd watched too many games. I always loved playing on Astroturf because it made me feel fast. I wasn't one of those guys blessed with a lot of speed so when I got on that turf, it was like when you were a kid and you put on those Pro Keds and all of a sudden they make you feel faster. That's what it was like at Texas Stadium. That turf made me feel like I was a kid again, I had my Pro Keds on, and I could really fly. Of course, what you fail to realize is that, hell, that guy you're trying to cover is faster, too.

I couldn't have any complaints about Texas Stadium simply because of what it meant to me to be there. It meant that I had arrived where I wanted to be. The dream manifested itself and not only for just being there. Coach Eddie Robinson always talked about, "Don't just wear the uniform, son. You've got to be something special. If you're going to wear the uniform, do something special in that uniform."

I had the unique experience of coming back to Texas Stadium as an opponent. That was crazy, the first game back after Jimmy Johnson got rid of me. I was coming back (in 1990) with the team (New York Giants) favored to win the Super Bowl. The Cowboys were still up and coming and you could tell they were going to be good. But it was weird, wearing a different uniform.

The Giants weren't intimidated by Texas Stadium, especially that year. There was no Tom Landry. All the ghosts were gone. The Pearsons, Dorsetts, all of them were gone and there was a new brand of players coming in. What touched me was that the Giants knew how big a game it was for them, not just because it was Texas Stadium, but the Cowboys at Texas Stadium.

Before the game coach (Bills) Parcells made a little talk because he wanted me to keep my head on straight. He said before the whole team that this game meant more to some guys than others and, of course, everyone knew who he was talking about. They knew what was going on, how much it meant to me. It was almost like they were trying to win the game for me.

The crowd cheered when I went on the field. It was like a home game for me. They announced Everson Walls and it was just the same, and it made me feel like I was home again. It was extremely straining because I felt like whether they were for the Cowboys or Giants, they were for me. The fans saw you as an individual. You just happened to be in a different uniform.

It's like a Cowboy fan once told me. He said I don't care about you going to the Giants and winning the Super Bowl with them. Just so long as the Giants know it took a Cowboy to get in front of the ball.

Remembering

TEXAS STADIUM

PRESTON PEARSON

(Running Back, 1975-80)

I only played against the Cowboys once prior to coming to Dallas and that was in the Cotton Bowl (1968) when I was with the Baltimore Colts. To be honest with you, I didn't know a whole lot more about the Cowboys when I was in Pittsburgh (1970-'74). I only played basketball in college (Illinois) so football wasn't really my longtime interest. I watched Chicago and Green Bay a little bit, but that was about it for the NFL.

I came to Dallas under a rather traumatic situation. I was let go by the Steelers and there were hard feelings. I felt like I was run out of town. I felt like they lied about the reasons they let me go. I was 30 years old, a seven-year veteran at the time. When you get up in that time frame and are let go it's tough to find a job.

My first important memory of Texas Stadium is the reception I received from the fans. Warming up for my first game there I felt how close the people were to the field. That's probably an advantage the Cowboys have at home. As some of our defensive guys where changing positions Jethro Pugh came up to me and said, "Hey, Prez,"—Jethro called me Prez from day one—and he pointed to some people who were holding up a sign in the stands.

It was one of those hand-written signs. To my surprise and to the credit of America's Team's fans, the sign said something to the effect, "Welcome,

Preston Pearson, #26."

Since I didn't know much about the Cowboys I wondered how these people knew enough about me to put up a sign with my name spelled correctly. I thought it was great. That made me feel settled in and like I was part of the team from day one. They made me feel welcome.

It was a great feeling to become an integral part of a team that ended up in the Super Bowl. Chuck Noll, the Pittsburgh coach, really shut me out from the moment players went on strike in '74. We went to his office to tell him what we as the Steelers were doing and as a head coach he should appreciate that we were sticking together as a team and not just as individual players out on strike.

I met the guy and he scared the hell out of me. My knees were shaking. He reared back in his chair, folded his hands behind his head and said something like, "What are you doing with my team?" From that moment forward I knew I didn't have a chance with the Steelers. He just didn't like me for being part of the strike as the player representative.

That gave Rocky Bleier a chance to stay with the team, but I was gone. I have no ill-will toward Rocky because he didn't have anything to do with it. He was just trying to get a job, too. But I disliked Chuck Noll for a long time after that . . . for years.

I found out later he said that I had something wrong with my knee. That was a lie. I never had anything wrong with my knee until I got hit in '78 or '79 out in Thousand Oaks. Noll just didn't appreciate me, didn't want me on the team, tried to find ways to get rid of me and finally had to lie to do it.

After 10 or 12 years I decided I had to let go of this anger. It was too much pressure on me to harbor ill will toward this idiot man. As it turned out, he just made a mistake and the mistake was to my advantage. Coming to Dallas certainly prolonged my career for another six years and gave me an opportunity to play for the great Tom Landry.

When Tony Dorsett arrived (1977) I held him off as long as I could. I knew he was going to start eventually. I knew from his abilities he was good. But Tony didn't want to catch passes or block or be in there on third down situations. Landry had come up with a shotgun formation (in '75) so while Dorsett was breaking in as a rookie, he took advantage of my ability to run precise routes, get open and catch the ball. I became a third down pass receiving specialist out of the backfield and if I remember right, no other

DALLAS

Preston Pearson

(RB, 1967-1980)

★ Five Super Bowl Appearances

★ Two-time Super Bowl Champion (1975, 1978)

★ Appeared in the Super Bowl with 3 different teams (Baltimore Colts, Pittsburgh Steelers, Dallas Cowboys)

★ Won Super Bowl championships with 2 different teams (Steelers, Cowboys)

★ 3,609 Career Rushing Yards

★ 3,095 Career Reception Yards

★ 2,801 Career Kickoff Return Yards

★ He also returned punts early in his career.

★ 33 Career TDs

★ Texas Black Sports Hall of Fame

★ Came to define the "third-down back," now commonly known as a "change-of-pace" back

★ Never played football in college, where instead he excelled in basketball

COWBOYS

team in the league was using a player like that.

I often wondered what the hell they were thinking by trying to cover me with a linebacker. Thomas Henderson was probably the toughest I had to go against and that was in practice. There was a linebacker in Washington, Monte Coleman, number 59, who was pretty good. He might have been the only one who gave me a little trouble. I always relished the fact that, OK, they're going to use a linebacker. That's fine.

A lot of teams would try to change up and put a safety out there, often a strong safety, who was a slow dude. They were even worse. You used your strength against them. Landry created that position for me so I tried to take full advantage of it every time I was out there.

My most memorable game at Texas Stadium had to be against the Redskins in '79 where we came from behind to score twice in the last four minutes. We were getting our butts kicked in the first half (behind 0-17). I scored our first touchdown (26 yards) on a pass from Roger Staubach. We went ahead (21-17) then fell behind again (34-21) and were still behind (34-28) when Larry Cole made the key play of the game. He stopped John Riggins on third down to get us going on our winning drive.

I think I had two critical catches on that drive, I recall Coleman was the guy I beat, and it topped off a nice game for me personally (five-for-108 yards receiving, one TD). Anyway, those plays helped get us close enough for Tony Hill to make the deciding touchdown catch (7 yards) that won the game (35-34).

I'll be sad to some degree to see Texas Stadium go because of the history and the memories we all have of playing there. But what is it—39 or 40 years old? It's old, it's dirty and it needed to

"My first important memory of Texas Stadium is the reception I received from the fans. Warming up for my first game there . . .Jethro Pugh came up . . . and pointed to some people who were holding up a sign in the stands. It said 'Welcome Preston Pearson, #26.' That made me feel welcome."

be updated. If they're going to be the Dallas Cowboys with this huge image they need a stadium that goes with the image. Right now Texas Stadium has probably seen its best days.

So mostly I'm looking forward to what the Cowboys are going to do with this monstrosity out there in Arlington. You know Jerry Jones has to have the best of everything and he'll probably have it with this new stadium for at least a little while. That is, until somebody tries to outdo him. Or he tries to outdo himself.

Remembering

TEXAS STADIUM

TONY
HILL

(Wide Reciever, 1977-86)

Two games at Texas Stadium come to mind beyond the dream-come-true feeling of stepping on that field for the first time. The first one is obvious—that 1979 game where we came back to win (35-34) over the Washington Redskins. The other is one that probably no one but me will remember.

The Washington game remains huge in my mind. It was Drew Pearson coming across the middle to make a catch under pressure. Ron Springs catching one to help position us for our final move. Me catching that last pass (7 yards for the winning TD) over Lemar Parrish. The intensity in the huddle was electric.

They came with man-to-man coverage on me and Parrish took an inside position. I'd beaten him on a couple of slant routes so he was right where I needed him to be. I dipped him inside and broke to the corner. Roger put the ball in a perfect place where I was the only one who had a chance to catch it. For almost 30 years, there's been a debate over why Staubach picked me as his receiver.

My recall is that I told Roger I could beat Parrish. Roger's version is that he told me before the ball was snapped to be alert. We still argue about who said what. As far as I'm concerned that's my story and I'm sticking to it.

163

My other memory is from a 1979 game (38-13) against the Cincinnati Bengals. I bet no one else can recall a single play from that Sunday. That's the reason it's special to me.

I was in bed that morning and my shoulder popped out of joint for about 45 minutes. I couldn't get out of bed or get dressed. Luckily my shoulder slipped back to normal and I raced to Texas Stadium. I didn't know how my shoulder would hold up. I was late. When I got to the game everyone was going out on the field. I did a quick change, hustled to the field with a sore shoulder and wound up having a great game. I ended up having five catches for about 75 yards and one touchdown. I did it all with one arm. That's why this game remains a personal favorite.

My freshman year at Stanford (1973) was Drew Pearson's rookie season with the Cowboys and their quarterback, Roger Staubach. I fantasized about playing with them. I was a quarterback in high school so (Joe) Namath was one of my guys. So was Sonny Jurgensen. But Roger was my idol.

This is a true story. The first time I met Roger I was like a kid. I told him, "Man, you're the greatest. You're my idol. I wore your Number 12 in high school. I've been watching you since I was in the third grade."

Roger gave me a look that would kill. Here I was pouring out my heart and he gave me a chilly stare. I didn't realize what I said must have sounded like I thought he was ancient. Then I had the same thing happen to me.

It was déjà vu years later when we were playing a preseason game and Danny White overthrew me with a pass. As I went to pick up the ball a defensive back got in my ear said, "Tony Hill, you're not going to believe this but I went to your same school and played quarterback. I've always wanted to meet you. I've been watching you since I was in the second grade."

I felt about 800 years old. I called Roger and told him, hey, I apologize for what I said about watching you since I was a kid. Now I knew how it made him feel. You know Roger. He just shook it off like it was nothing. But it proved without question that what goes around comes around.

My introduction to the NFL included a scene I found hard to believe. I saw these little ashtrays in the locker room and thought that was where

DALLAS

Tony Hill

(WR, 1977-1986)

★ Two Super Bowl Appearances

★ Super Bowl Champion (1978)

★ Selected to the Pro Bowl three times

★ 479 Career Receptions

★ 7,988 Career Pass Reception Yards

★ 51 Career TDs

★ Also returned punts and kickoffs briefly in his career

★ Third-round draft pick out of Stanford University

COWBOYS

> "There's one side of me that says I will miss Texas Stadium as a player when it's gone. But . . . Texas Stadium has been there for 1,400 years and these younger guys want to move on and start their own tradition. History doesn't repeat itself, so you have to move on."

you put your change, car keys and stuff like that. I didn't know players smoked. I didn't see it in training camp. But we'd go in at halftime and Jethro (Pugh), (Ralph) Neely and (John) Fitzgerald would fire up!

What is this? It freaked me out. This is weird. I thought those ashtrays were a change holder or a cup holder but these guys are using them to break out cigarettes!

Before we say so long to Texas Stadium, I have a major complaint. I think it's unfortunate that what Drew and I accomplished as wide receivers is not recognized. It was an incredible feat. He and I were the first pair of NFC receivers on the same team to gain more than 1,000 yards in the same season. (Hill had 1,062 yards and 10 touchdown catches; Pearson 1026 yards and eight TDs in 1979). Considering what we accomplished there's no question we should be considered for the Pro Football Hall of Fame.

There's one side of me that says I will miss Texas Stadium as a player when it's gone. But leaving Texas Stadium is like when we left that ancient tub or motor home practice place over on Forest Lane and moved to Valley Ranch (in 1985). Valley Ranch was incredible in comparison, a night and day difference. Texas Stadium has been there for 1,400 years and these younger guys want to move on and start their own tradition. That's what it's all about.

Sports are for the youth, and times change. History doesn't repeat itself so you have to move on. From a selfish standpoint you're going to miss Texas Stadium but as a player you know how to put things in perspective. This move to Arlington is going to be the best thing that could happen to the Cowboys.

The worst thing was that the mayor of Dallas had no foresight. The Cowboys should be playing in downtown Dallas.

Remembering

TEXAS STADIUM

CLIFF HARRIS

(Free Safety, 1970-79)

Before the Cowboys moved to Texas Stadium, we played in traditional stadiums around the NFL and coming from Ouachita Baptist, everything looked awesome to me. Even the high school stadiums impressed me.

I remember the Los Angeles Coliseum and San Diego as dramatic. We'd also played in the Astrodome. Just walking into Texas Stadium was imposing because it was closed except for the hole in the roof. It locked you in. The Cotton Bowl that we left was similar to the stadiums of the time. The fans were right on top of you. They'd come down to the bench, you could turn around and talk to them.

Texas Stadium was definitely more removed. It matched Tom Landry's personality to keep a distance. There was a 10-12 foot wall between the ground floor and the fans. That kept them back from you. But the stadium also defined our team because it was first class and a snazzy first one of its kind. It was perfect for us, blue and silver, shiny and slick.

What I liked about Texas Stadium is that the field was crowned more than most. It was an easier field for a free safety to play on. When you lined up at midfield it meant you were running downhill to meet a running back turning up field. So you had the advantage. And if you hit a receiver who was up against the sideline there was more impact.

It was also easier to triangulate from that crown. Let me explain. It is easier to stand on top of a hill, so to say, and analyze where a deep pass is going because you have an angle. You can determine where the sidelines are a lot better from there. Then take Busch Stadium in St. Louis, a baseball park. It was flat. The fans were 30 yards away. You'd look out there and couldn't tell where the sidelines were. At Texas Stadium I knew exactly where the sideline was. It defined the area I had to cover a lot better.

I had a reputation as a hard hitter. Also, as a player who preferred force more than finesse. Over the years my longtime safety partner, Charlie Waters, tried to simplify my play by using a force over finesse comparison, which made me the force and him finesse. That wasn't the case in reality.

I was a logical player, a technician. If I saw a receiver who I could hit and knock out of the game early and I knew that play would be reflected in all the films receivers studied the rest of the year, I'd hit him. Of course, I wouldn't do that if it was third-and-10 and we were behind.

If you step in front of a receiver and intercept a pass, he'll be a little upset. But if you blast him and turn his helmet around then he'll be looking for you. I get a bigger charge out of doing it that way. Then I talk to the receiver and ask him, "Is it worth it?"

There's a risk-hero component involved. Do you tackle somebody or take the chance to intercept and miss the ball, they catch it and go for a touchdown and win the game? Or do you just knock the guy out?

Lots of guys have glory in their eyes rather than victory. They don't play for the team or for victory. They play for themselves. I always played to win with the team in mind. Sometimes I knocked the ball down when others would try to pick it off. Those others could lose the game because they went for the pick.

I recall the shadows at Texas Stadium for a good reason. People probably don't remember but I was the first to return punts and kickoffs there when it opened in '71. Go look it up. I averaged 28.4 yards on 29 kickoff returns. No Cowboy since with as many or more attempts has beaten my average.

Two things happened on punt returns, and both were confusing. If the ball was kicked out of darkness, you backpedaled into bright light and it was like, oh, my gosh, where's the ball? The reverse was true if you back pedaled from a bright area into the darkness. Where did it go?

DALLAS

Cliff Harris

(DB, 1970-1979)

★ Five Super Bowl Appearances

★ Two-time Super Bowl Champion (1972, 1978)

★ Selected to the Pro Bowl six times

★ Named All-Pro four times

★ Named to the NFL's 1970 All-Decade Team

★ Ring of Honor (2004)

★ 29 Career Interceptions

★ Nicknamed "Captain Crash" for his reckless pursuit of ball carriers from his safety position

★ Also returned punts and kickoffs early in his career

★ Was a free agent acquisition out of NAIA school Quachita Baptist College.

★ Arkansas Sports Hall of Fame

★ NAIA Hall of Fame.

COWBOYS

I've been asked who nicknamed me "Captain Crash." There never was a Captain Crash ever. That came later. Our linebacker Dave Edwards called me Crash, but certainly not Captain Crash because there was only one captain and that was Staubach. It didn't stop Golden Richards from his gag of presenting me with a yellow crash helmet featuring a siren and flashing red light on top.

I kind of let the Captain Crash label go on over the years. The only thing that upsets me is when people call me Captain Crunch. That's a cereal! And I don't even like it.

> "The stadium defined our team because it was first class and a snazzy first one of its kind. It was perfect for us, blue and sliver, shiny and slick."

Another question I've gotten over the years was to name the running backs who hit me the hardest. Earl Campbell (Houston) was the toughest. John Riggins (Washington) didn't get as much acclaim as Campbell but he hit hard and he was fast, too. Larry Csonka (Miami) didn't hit as hard but tackling him was like trying to pull down a moving house or trying to stop a slow-moving elephant. You could only finally get him if you tied two legs together.

I feel fortunate to be able to reminisce considering I was an obscure free agent from a small college in Arkansas. The Saints and Rams talked to me, but that was all they did. So did a combine of five other NFL teams. The Cowboys came to the campus a couple of times and timed me. I ran a 4.4 or 4.5 on grass in football shoes. Gil Brandt told me the Cowboys would draft me in the top six rounds.

I hung by the phone all day. Everybody in Ouachita knew about it and kept asking when I'd been drafted. Gil called about midnight and said the Cowboys were coming to sign me the next day. No, you're not, I told him, because I was very upset. But then, none of the other teams called that night or had offered a contract.

I talked to my coach the next day and he recommended I sign with the team that showed the most interest which was the Cowboys, and it turned out fine. Besides I liked their pants. They were shiny and unique in the NFL because everyone else wore grey, green or black.

My thoughts as a long odds rookie to stick with a team that went to Super Bowl V went like this: First, I told myself I got to go to training camp. Then I told myself at least I got to stay around and see the veterans. And then at least I was around for the first preseason game. And so forth.

Now it's 30-something years later and Texas Stadium is on the way out. I'm an emotional, passionate person. Jim Hart (former St. Louis quarterback), a great nemesis back then and a great friend today, sent me a tape of the demolition of Busch Stadium. He added a note that said, "Doesn't this make you feel old?"

Some of the best places to play were historic like Yankee Stadium. You can feel the energy of the past there. RFK Stadium in Washington was a dramatic place to play, the most fun, but we don't play there anymore. There were also places that caused lots of trauma, and that would be Busch Stadium, the hardest place for me to play.

Losing Texas Stadium will be like seeing a home you grew up in as a kid demolished. The first time I drive by where it once stood and see that it's not there anymore will make an emotional impact on me.

Remembering

TEXAS STADIUM

CHARLIE WATERS

(Defensive Back, 1970-78, 1980-81)

My favorite place to play was Texas Stadium and on the road it was RFK Stadium in Washington because of what we did to the fans when we beat the Redskins. We shut them up. That was sweet.

Texas Stadium is like a little dollhouse with a college atmosphere. The stadium is so intimate. There's not a bad seat in the house. You can hear what the fans are yelling on the field. Athletes are motivated by vocal fans so that was one of the aspects that I liked about Texas Stadium.

The Cotton Bowl was good as a home field but all the noise went up in the air. But it hovered at Texas Stadium because of that partial roof. It felt warm and intimate there, and truly a home field advantage. I was very comfortable playing there.

I remember the first time we went to Texas Stadium to practice because it was raining. When it rained coach Landry always took us to a field with artificial turf. I guess it was for the New England game (Texas Stadium opener). Coach Landry wanted us to see what the field was like in case it rained on Sunday.

There was a break in the practice when I heard someone holler, "Hey, Muddy. Come over here!"

I knew who was being called. It was me. I also knew who was

calling. It was Cornell Green, who always called me Muddy Waters. A funny guy, he was leaning against the stadium wall around the 40-yard line. I walked over and took off my helmet. Knowing Cornell, he might have been smoking a cigarette.

"Is this (bleeped) or what?" he grumbled. "When it's rainin' like hell all the fans are going to be dry and we'll be getting wet. That ain't right."

I agreed it was strange. Cornell kept complaining, "That ain't right," which was his catchall phrase for whatever he didn't like.

My first overall perception of Texas Stadium was the glitter. There was lots of it. It seemed so flashy. The first time I drove over for a game I saw Texas Stadium from a distance and thought to myself, hell, this is nothing more than a giant silver hamburger in the sky with a flat top.

I learned over time to appreciate the nuances of Texas Stadium. I loved the tunnel. I thought it was cool. We played in lots of stadiums that didn't have the drama of that tunnel where you can hear the excitement out there and visualize what it's going to be like. Texas Stadium was great at creating that type effect.

You didn't get that reaction in other stadiums. You'd have to meander around some of those old stadiums, duck under pipes and other stuff to get to the field. I still have an emotional bond with that tunnel in Texas Stadium. It means a lot to me even now when I walk down it. I get little chills even after 30 years. It reminds me of what I felt like when I was standing there before a game.

Even though I tore up my knee on artificial turf I'd rather play on it than grass because it's predictable. You know what you're dealing with even when it's wet. I don't want variables. I want constants. Artificial turf is a constant. The variables are those little wide receivers.

Yet there's a memorable game where Texas Stadium turf played false with me. It was during a divisional playoff loss (14-12) to the Rams in '76. I'd already blocked one punt when I went to the sideline to talk to coach Landry or (defensive coordinator) Ernie Stautner. We were behind 14-10 and Roger Staubach came over to chirp about getting the ball back.

"Don't worry," I told him. "We'll get it back. We only need one score. I'm going to block the next punt and run it back for a touchdown."

Of course, I had no idea I'd do that. I was trying to talk myself into it.

Well, I did block the punt. Texas Stadium's turf was hard and usually the ball bounced pretty high off of it. This time the ball rolled downhill off

DALLAS

Charlie Waters

(DB, 1970-78, 1980-81)

★ Five Super Bowl Appearances

★ Two-time Super Bowl Champion (1972, 1978)

★ Selected to the Pro Bowl three times

★ Voted All-Conference three times

★ Selected All-NFL six times

★ 41 Career Interceptions

★ 4 Consecutive Games With an Interception rank second in team history

★ 9 Career Playoff Interceptions are a team record

★ 3 interceptions in a playoff game against Chicago (1977) are a team record

★ 2 fumble recoveries in a playoff game against Detroit (1970) are a team record

★ In a 1976 poll of players, Sports Illustrated named him the most underrated and unsung player in the NFL

COWBOYS

that high crown on the field as I stalked it. I kept thinking it would bring itself up on a bounce. It never did.

The turf abandoned me. The ball wound up rolling out of bounds. I didn't pick it up and run for a touchdown. (Laughs) Now Roger blames me for losing the game because I told him that's what I was going to do.

> "I loved the tunnel. I thought it was cool. We played in lots of stadiums that didn't have the drama of that tunnel, where you can hear the excitement out there and visualize what it's going to be like. It means a lot to me even now when I walk down it. I get little chills even after 30 years."

I performed in playoff games. That's what you're judged by. Look at the playoff records and I'm in there.

Another game that sticks in my mind is one where I didn't play. I was a radio analyst with play-by-play announcer Brad Sham when the Cowboys won that 35-34 thriller against Washington in '79. Everyone gave up except me. I kept saying, "You gotta believe!" Fans were going home. Brad gave up. But I never wavered. Sure enough we began a comeback. I always believed we would win.

My NFL career was a series of comebacks, some from a broken arm, knee surgery and shoulder injuries. Of course, I had to come back from being cut by the Cowboys before my rookie season began.

I was in my room at the Holiday Inn on Central Expressway when coach Jim Myers called. He told me to bring my playbook and report to coach Landry in about two hours. I knew what that meant. I was out. About an hour later Myers called back to say they'd made a mistake. I didn't count against the roster yet. Because I'd played in the College All-Star game I had an exemption.

"What? Are you (bleeping) me?" I said to Myers.

"Hey, you don't talk to me like that!" he snapped.

I should have said, don't be jerking my heart around. But I didn't. The next week I had a good game so they gambled on keeping me.

I had some rough times early in my career at cornerback, a position that didn't fit my talent. Strong safety was my natural position and where I began to earn Pro Bowl and All-Pro recognition. Me as a cornerback was like asking Lee Roy Jordan to play strong safety. He didn't have the body for it. He was smart. But he didn't have the speed. That was pretty much what I was. I had good speed and the body for strong safety. But I was the wrong body type at the corner.

Texas Stadium is a special place, like a college atmosphere. It's a warm, fuzzy stadium. And a deadly home field advantage. I have lots of fond memories of where I played my whole career, pulled myself up and was part of something so successful. It'll mean something to me when it's gone.

From a player's point of view, even opposing players recognized our home field advantage. It was loud. The fans were part of the game. Emotion plays such a huge role in a game. I don't know if they'll get that at the new stadium. But they sure had it at Texas Stadium.

Some wonder whether tradition will transfer to the stadium in Arlington. You would think not. But when we moved from the Cotton Bowl to Texas Stadium, everything moved intact. It worked fine. It's just part of the progression.

Remembering

TEXAS STADIUM

MY 10 MOST MEMORABLE GAMES

By Frank Luksa

Since the 2008 season will be the 38th and last at Texas Stadium as home field for the Arlington-bound Dallas Cowboys, a personal reminisce is in order. Distant replay means that I have chosen my 10 most memorable games since the Irving complex opened on October 24, 1971.

I have seen virtually every game there and reduced more than 300 of them into this compact list. Since they were mine, the qualifying rules were simple. Inclusion demanded a gee-whiz result so extraordinary that it had never been seen before and likely would never to be seen again. The event also became Top 10 material because, well, I said so.

Those parameters eliminated seemingly worthy candidates such as the 2002 game where Emmitt Smith broke Walter Payton's NFL career rushing record. Even as an historical achievement, Smith was certain to do it, so the moment lacked shock value. The same goes for the 1985 game when Chicago Bears coach Mike Ditka, a former Cowboys player and assistant coach, returned to lead a 44-0 rout. Other than noting that their consecutive scoring streak at 218 games had ended, elaborating on the Cowboys seemed pointless.

I also reluctantly tossed the last game of 1989, the maiden season of the Jones-Johnson era. The Cowboys lost their seventh game in a row on a sub-freezing afternoon. Recall, my criteria for Top 10 honors required a would-you-believe-it reaction. This one threatened to qualify because for the first time in Texas Stadium history it was so cold that . . .

Toilets froze.

Therefore it was necessary to combine the frigid scene with a 1-15 finish in a few picturesque words for a newspaper column. Thus I wrote:

The 1989 season was so awful it wouldn't even flush.

But I digress. My list of Top 10 Games . . .

1—DALLAS 35, WASHINGTON 34
(Dec. 16, 1979)

Roger Staubach's 7-yard fade route touchdown to Tony Hill with 0:39 left applied his last he's-done-it-again finish. It was the 21st game Staubach won in the fourth quarter, 14 of them in the final two minutes.

The game was start-to-finish wild. Washington scored the first 17 points, Dallas the next 21, Washington 17 more in succession before the Cowboy claimed the final 14. Larry Cole made the most famous tackle in Texas Stadium history, a third down stop of John Riggins that kept the Redskins from freezing their 34-28 lead.

Staubach's Hall of Fame career ended on a weird note one week later during a 21-19 playoff loss to the Los Angeles Rams. He completed his last NFL pass to guard Herb Scott, an ineligible receiver.

2—DALLAS 24, WASHINGTON 23
(Nov. 28, 1974)

"We put Staubach out and all they've got is that (Clint) Longley kid," predicted Redskins defensive tackle Diron Talbert, unaware that answered prayers can boomerang.

The Redskins did put Staubach out with a concussion early in the third quarter. Rookie Longley, nicknamed "The Mad Bomber" for bouncing passes off Tom Landry's coaching tower in training camp, inherited a hopeless looking 16-3 deficit. Yet he won the game with a stunning 50-yard touchdown pass to Drew Pearson with less than a minute left.

"I was in the huddle when he called basically the last play of the game, and we all knew it wouldn't work," recalled fullback Walt Garrison. "Who's going to throw a 50-yard pass for a touchdown? They'll have Drew covered like a blanket. He'll probably throw a five-yard out to me or Duane

Thomas and hope we can run for a touchdown. Hell, I hadn't run 40 yards in my life."

Longley's only claim to NFL fame was immortalized by guard Blaine Nye, who analyzed his heroics as, "A triumph of the uncluttered mind."

3—MIAMI 16, DALLAS 14
(Nov. 25, 1993)

A day frozen in time as the most bizarre home loss. It began with a freak sleet and snow storm that left the field glazed. It ended when Leon Lett's brain iced over.

A blocked Miami field goal sealed an apparent 14-13 Dallas victory with mere seconds on the clock. The still-in-play ball rolled toward the Cowboys end zone with Dallas players waving their arms in warning not to touch it.

For purposes unknown to this day, Lett ignored them and slid into the ball. Whatever his muddled intent he punched the ball to the 1-yard line where Miami recovered, kicked a 19-yard field goal and beat the bewildered Cowboys with 0:03 left to play.

"There were 11 men on the field and 10 of them knew what to do," sighed special teams coach Joe Avazzano.

4—DALLAS 42, GREEN BAY 31
(Nov. 24, 1994)

With Troy Aikman and Rodney Peete hurt, third-string free agent quarterback Jason Garrett was the only overmatched option left to start against Brett Favre.

Hence there was no surprise when the Packers intercepted Garrett's first pass and led at halftime 17-6. This was second year Garrett's first NFL start. He'd been inactive for the first 10 games of the season and in near mint condition thereafter since he'd thrown a total of five passes that gained four yards.

What followed has never been explained except in supernatural terms. Garrett produced five touchdowns in fewer than 19 minutes of the second half. That's his signature on a franchise record 36 points scored post-intermission. He finished with 311 yards passing, two touchdowns and somewhat dazed by what he'd done.

"If this is a fairy tale, so be it," he said.

5—PHILADELPHIA 27, DALLAS 0
(Nov. 23, 1989)

The Bounty Bowl originated with kicker Luis Zendejas, who claimed Eagles coach Buddy Ryan offered $200 to knock him out of the game and $500 for a kayo of Troy Aikman.

Zendejas said he taped the threats during a telephone chat with an unidentified source but never produced it for anyone to hear. It didn't matter since it was easier to cast Ryan as a villain who'd previously ordered a rub-it-in touchdown against Tom Landry and insulted Jimmy Johnson as a suspect NFL head coaching hire.

"Tell Jimmy there won't be any East Carolinas or Cincinnatis on his schedule," Ryan needled the former University of Miami coach when he replaced Landry.

Even after Ryan pulled his regulars late in the game, Johnson was furious at the final gun. He bolted to midfield looking for the long-gone Ryan.

"I would have said something to Buddy but he wouldn't stand on the field long enough. He got his fat rear end into the dressing room," Johnson snapped.

NFL commissioner Paul Tagliabue's investigation predictably cleared the Eagles from plotting naughty things against the Cowboys. The feud left curious minds to wonder what might happen during a Jimmy-Buddy rematch later in Philadelphia.

"Will they shake hands or arm wrestle?" pondered Dave Widell of the Cowboys. Actually nothing unusual occurred unless this was the game where Eagles fans pelted Johnson with snow balls (batteries included).

6—DALLAS 38, CINCINNATI 10
(Nov. 4, 1973)

The greatest show by a middle linebacker somehow slipped into virtual obscurity. Lee Roy Jordan intercepted three passes from Ken Anderson and returned one 31 yards for a touchdown, a remarkable feat for a defensive back much less a linebacker.

Jordan's triple exceeds the mere remarkable. All of his interceptions were made in the first quarter! But there is more to tell. All of those picks were made within the span of five minutes! I checked old game story accounts to verify details—surely an NFL record for most interceptions in the least amount of time.

Lee Roy made 32 career interceptions, an extraordinarily high total for a linebacker. Curiosity led me to call the keeper of all records, the Elias Sports Bureau, to check how that ranked all-time among linebackers.

Jordan's 32 tied him with Nick Buoniconti of Miami and Jack Ham of Pittsburgh. The leader is Don Shinnick of Baltimore with 37, followed by Stan White, who played for Baltimore and Detroit and had 34.

Jordan, who last played 31 years ago, still ranks No. 7 on the Cowboys all-time interception list. You will find him listed above a couple of defensive backs named Cliff Harris (29) and Darren Woodson (23).

7—DALLAS 38, SAN FRANCISCO 21
(Jan. 3, 1994)

Jimmy Johnson did something before this NFC Championship Game that no other coach ever did or ever thought about doing.

First, he called a local radio sports talk show. Coaches never volunteer for those programs. They're the outlet where goobers complain that the coach is an idiot who can't motivate foam to rise.

Johnson then announced to a baffled talk show host and a stunned audience that the Cowboys would beat the 49ers! I never heard a coach that brave, over-wired or stupid to predict victory in public.

"We will win the ball game!" Johnson guaranteed. "You can put that in three-inch high headlines!"

What made Johnson pop off? Some thought his bravado could have been Heineken fueled. Most knew that Johnson was cocky and always ultra-confident. I recall asking him if the Cowboys might not have been so successful without Troy Aikman.

"They'd still have me," he half joked.

San Francisco coach George Seifert considered Johnson's brag with admiration and bemusement.

"Well, the man has balls, I'll say that," Seifert began. "I don't know if they're brass or paper mache. We'll find out."

He found out they were brass.

8—SAN FRANCISCO 41, COWBOYS 24
(Sept. 24, 2000)

George Teague became captain of my All-Hero Team for tangling with a visiting peacock. He knocked Terrell Owens on his butt. It was the most redeeming tackle since of the locals blind-sided Joe Theismann.

It occurred after Owens caught his second touchdown pass and celebrated by racing to midfield, where he posed astride the Cowboys star emblem with arms upraised. A blur of blue interrupted the scene and left Owens sprawled on his pompous rear. That was Teague, the only Cowboy with enough chest hair to retaliate with the 49ers ahead, 41-17.

"The first time it was, 'OK, you got us. You got your hurrahs,' " said Teague. "But to go back again is where you cross the line. Then it becomes disrespectful.

"We were losing by three touchdowns, maybe four. It was about 145 degrees on the turf and nothing was going our way. I had an intuition that if Owens scored again he'd do something crazy. I made up my mind that if he scores again and grandstands there'll be a fight. Before I knew it I whacked Owens pretty good. What I really appreciated was being quick enough to duck a 300-pounder who then went after me."

Since Owens signed with the Cowboys, no one harps on the incident.

9—DALLAS 44, NEW ENGLAND 21
(Oct. 24, 1971)

Texas Stadium opened to popular acclaim from everyone except the players. Three complaints arose about the 65,000-seat facility that owner Clint Murchison, Jr., built in Irving.

First, the field was too hard. Second, fans who bought bonds to help finance the stadium and those seated in $50,000 Circle Suites were too aristocratic to make much noise. Their on-high presence conjured an image of the Roman Coliseum among the players.

"Our concept of football was more like the Cotton Bowl with the crowd outside and involved," said Larry Cole. "You didn't watch a football game with a coat and tie on from a box."

Finally, fans were protected from the elements by an overhang but players beneath the hole in the roof weren't.

"Hell, if Clint wanted us to fight the elements why didn't he just roof the joint over and put in a sprinkler system?" Charlie Waters wondered.

Murchison's price of $50,000 for a Circle Suite was originally hooted as absurdly overpriced. In retrospect they were among the best real estate investments in north Texas. Some resold a few years later for $500,000 and up.

10

The reason there is no score for this December game in 1991 is because I spent that Sunday afternoon disoriented and don't remember a thing that happened on the field.

My state of shock occurred as I was on my way to work and heard that I was out of work. En route to the game I listened to a radio bulletin announce that my newspaper, the *Dallas Times Herald,* would cease publication on Monday.

Only later did I realize how the shutdown gifted me with a rare triple play. I became the only columnist to have worked for all three major metropolitan newspapers—*Fort Worth Star-Telegram, Times Herald* and later, the *Dallas Morning News*—and had helped put only one out of business.

Other than adding that plum on my resume, the timing of the shutdown was inconvenient. I'd planned to ask for a raise on Tuesday.

Remembering

TEXAS STADIUM

TEXAS STADIUM

Location: Irving, Texas
Style: Outdoor
Cost of Construction: $35 million
Playing Surface: Artificial (1971-80, Tartan Turf; 1981-95, Tartan Turf; 1996-2002, RealGrass; 2002-2008, Tufted Nylon 6)
Original Seating Capacity: 65,101
Current Seating Capacity: 65,529
Original Number of Luxury Suites: 178
Current Number of Luxury Suites: 380
Size of the Hole in the Roof: Approximately 2.25 acres
First Event: Billy Graham Crusade, Sept. 17-26, 1971
First Game: October 24, 1971
First Opponent: New England Patriots
First TD Scored: Cowboys RB Duane Thomas scored on a 56-yard run vs. the Patriots less than three minutes into the game.
First Victory: 44-21 vs. New England Patriots on October 24, 1971
Attendance for First Game: 65,708
Overall Record: (1971-2007; 37 seasons): 207-98 (.679)
Playoff Record: 16-6 (.727)
Ring of Honor Members: Bob Lilly, Don Meredith, Don Perkins, Chuck Howley, Mel Renfro, Roger Staubach, Lee Roy Jordan, Tom Landry, Tony Dorsett, Randy White, Bob Hayes, Tex Schramm, Cliff Harris, Rayfield Wright, Troy Aikman, Michael Irvin, Emmitt Smith.
Super Bowl Championships: (5), 1971, 1977, 1992, 1993, 1995
Other Former Tenants: Dallas Tornado (soccer); SMU (football), University of North Texas (football)
Selected Other Events Held at Texas Stadium: 1973 NFL Pro Bowl; Religious Events (Billy Graham Crusade, Promise Keepers Conference, concert by Carmen); Musical Concerts (Paul McCartney, Eagles, Garth Brooks, George Strait and many others); Dirt Events (Supercross, Monster Trucks); Wrestling (World Championship Wrestling); Lacrosse (Major League Lacrosse); Hispanic Festivals (Cinco de Mayo, Diez Y Seis holidays); Car Shows; Festivals; Carnivals; College Football (Big XII Championship, various regular-season games); High School Football (Texas State Championship games, various regular-season and playoff games).

(Dallas Cowboys and www.DallasCowboys.com)